think deeply and flourish

A PRACTICAL GUIDE TO HAPPINESS

WILL BUCKINGHAM

This edition published in the UK
in 2018 by Icon Books Ltd,
Omnibus Business Centre,
39–41 North Road,
London N7 9DP
email: info@iconbooks.com
www.iconbooks.com

First published in the UK
in 2012 by Icon Books

Sold in the UK, Europe and Asia
by Faber & Faber Ltd,
Bloomsbury House,
74–77 Great Russell Street,
London WC1B 3DA
or their agents

Distributed in South Africa
by Jonathan Ball,
Office B4, The District,
41 Sir Lowry Road,
Woodstock 7925

Distributed in Australia and
New Zealand
by Allen & Unwin Pty Ltd,
PO Box 8500,
83 Alexander Street,
Crows Nest,
NSW 2065

Distributed in Canada
by Publishers Group Canada,
76 Stafford Street, Unit 300
Toronto,
Ontario M6J 2S1

Distributed in the USA
by Publishers Group West,
1700 Fourth Street,
Berkeley, CA 94710

ISBN: 978-178578-324-1

Typeset in Avenir by Marie Doherty

Printed and bound in the UK by Clays Ltd, St Ives plc

About the author

Will Buckingham is a freelance philosopher and writer. He is the author of several novels and philosophy books, as well as books for children. He has a PhD in philosophy from Staffordshire University. He has taught both philosophy and creative writing at universities in the UK, China and Myanmar. He currently lives in Leicester in the UK.

Contents

Part III: Beyond Happiness

Introduction:
the secret of happiness?

In brief
We might think that we want to be happy, or that we want to discover the secret of a happy life, but what do we mean when we say this? In this introductory chapter, we will look at three fundamental questions about happiness. Firstly, 'What is happiness?'; secondly, 'What makes us happy?'; and finally, 'Is there more to life than happiness?'

A secret of happiness?

Today, happiness is a booming industry. Where once psychologists were concerned with cataloguing mental illnesses and all the things that might go wrong with our minds, today they can often be found talking about things like character strengths, virtues and how we might lead the good life. Where economists once concerned themselves only with their balance sheets, these days they write about happiness as an indicator of the state of the nation. Even politicians are getting in on the act, proclaiming that they're in the business not only of building wealthy nations, but also of building *happy* nations. And if you go to your local bookshop, you'll find countless books promising you that, if you only part with your hard-earned cash, nestling within those pages you'll find the secret of happiness itself.

Introducing Happiness is not one of those books. This isn't because I know the secret of happiness but out of mean-spiritedness would rather keep it to myself. It's because there's something a bit suspect in the idea that there's any such thing as *the* secret of happiness. Instead this is a book about what happiness might be, about why it matters to us, about the problems with happiness, and about how some of the best philosophical minds of the past have not only asked questions about what happiness is, but also provided various kinds of tools and advice to help us live happier lives.

The first thing that this book aims to do, then, is to ask some tricky (but interesting) questions about the nature of happiness. When we start to look more closely at happiness, we'll find that it's a much more complicated business than we might have first thought. Even asking an apparently simple question like 'Am I happy now?' can start to tie us up in all kinds of knots and puzzles.

Think of the last time you felt happy (or, if you're happy now, pay attention to this happiness). Now ask yourself some of the questions below:

1. What kind of thing is happiness? Is it a physical feeling, a state of mind, or an emotion? Is it all of these things?

Or is it something different? How, in other words, do you know that you're happy?

2. Can you be both happy and unhappy at the same time? Can you be happy but dissatisfied?

3. Are you always aware of how happy you are? Does it make sense, for example, to say, 'I was happy, but I didn't know it'?

If you ask these questions with an inquiring mind, and ask them repeatedly, you might start to suspect that it's not always very clear what we mean by 'happy'. And the more you think about them, the more the questions around happiness seem to multiply.

However, this book isn't just about *theoretical* questions. Happiness matters to us not just in theory but also in practice; and so this book aims to find practical solutions to some of the puzzles around the different ideas of happiness.

 You can do the practical exercises in this book on your own; but it might be more interesting, and more fun, to find a friend so that you can explore some of these exercises together, and so you can discuss the questions raised along the way.

Happiness clearly matters to us, and the very fact that you picked up this book suggests that you have not only a theoretical interest in happiness, but also what philosophers sometimes call an *existential* interest in happiness. In other words, you want to know about happiness because happiness is something that you aspire to, something that matters not just in the abstract, but for your very *existence*.

Three questions

When it comes to philosophical approaches to happiness, among the many questions that we might ask, there are perhaps three that stand out. The first, and the most obvious, has already been hinted at: *What is happiness?* Is happiness a matter of being satisfied with our life? Is it a matter of pleasure? Or is it about having a life that's fulfilling? A little thought shows that these things don't always coincide. I might recognize, for example, that my life isn't particularly fulfilling at the moment, but I might be satisfied with it nevertheless. Or I might have a life filled with pleasure, but feel strangely dissatisfied. Or else I might think that pleasure really isn't that important, but care a great deal about fulfilment.

KEY FIGURE To see how complicated the question of happiness is, you only have to think about the Danish philosopher Søren Kierkegaard (1813–55) who, agonizing over his decision whether to marry or

4

not, decided that in the long run he would be 'happier in his unhappiness' if he didn't marry. So he didn't. Kierkegaard is associated in particular with the philosophical movement known as 'existentialism', and his books are well known for their strangeness and their extraordinary literary style.

Recent research, incidentally, suggests that Kierkegaard's decision may not have been the best gamble, and that the married tend to be happier, at least in a limited sense, than the never-married. However, before you use this as a reason to propose, the divorced fare rather *worse* than the never-married: you have been warned.

Leaving aside the issue of marital advice, here I want to focus on the apparent contradiction in the idea that you could be *happy in your unhappiness*. What does this mean? Are happiness and unhappiness mutually exclusive? Is Kierkegaard happy in one sense and unhappy in another? Is this a contradiction in terms? And, had Kierkegaard made the opposite decision, might he have gone on to be *unhappy in his happiness*?

The most important lesson we can draw from this, of course, is that it's best, if at all possible, not to become romantically involved with philosophers. But another lesson is that happiness is by no means straightforward, and that perhaps the word 'happiness' (not to mention 'joy', 'pleasure', 'cheerfulness', 'good cheer' and so on) may mean all kinds of things in all kinds of different contexts.

This question about what happiness actually *is*, is one that has preoccupied philosophers for centuries, and they are still arguing over how best to define it. Even if we can't resolve these arguments, if we're going to explore happiness at all, it will be useful to be aware of some of the philosophical problems that have been raised down the ages. So the first section of this book, called 'What is Happiness?', will look at some of the theoretical problems that we encounter when it comes to thinking about happiness. Along the way, I will be asking you to engage in various thought-experiments to help the philosophy along: these don't require you to leave the comfort of your armchair, but nevertheless demand that you think through the issues for yourself.

The second question that we need to ask about happiness arises out of the first, and that is: *What makes us happy?* The way we go about answering this question will depend, to some extent, on the way that we choose to answer the first question. It was George Bernard Shaw who famously said that you should *not* do to others as you would wish to be done to – the famous 'golden rule' of moral philosophy – because *they might have other tastes*. Perhaps your idea of fun is mortifying the flesh in a hillside hut, sleeping on a bed of nails and drinking only thin gruel; or perhaps you think that the ultimate happiness involves a couch, several bunches of grapes, a quantity of wine, and a gaggle of willing acolytes to tend to your every bodily need. One of the challenges of thinking and talking philosophically about happiness is that of being able to account for this human variation. But as much as we're different and unique, we're all in many ways the same; so despite Shaw's warnings, we might expect that, in general at least, there are some broad principles that we can discover about happiness and how it might occur.

 To explore happiness as fully as possible, we need to think not only about how different we are from each other, but also about how much we share and how we're often alike.

When it comes to these broad principles, however, I don't want you to take my word for it. After all, it's your life and your happiness, and if you really want to explore these questions, you'll need to do it yourself. So the second part of this book is called 'What Makes Us Happy?' and is more directly practical than the first part. Think of the second part as a series of practical experiments in happiness, drawn from the philosophers of the past. These experiments may sometimes require you to get up out of your philosophical armchair and actually try things out. In this part of the book, I will be drawing on philosophical and practical approaches to happiness from the pleasure-loving Epicurean philosophers to the strange Chinese vagabond Zhuangzi, from practices of Buddhist meditation to the practical wisdom of Aristotle. Being experiments, *not all of these approaches may work.* It's up to you to see what works and what doesn't. Nevertheless, some kind of first-person experience is essential if you want to really get to grips with the questions in this book.

 Many of the practical approaches we will explore here represent not only different approaches to happiness, but also different ideas of what happiness might be and what the 'good life' might look like.

In the third part of the book, called 'Beyond Happiness', I will be looking at a final question: *Is there more to life than happiness?* After all, it's perfectly possible to imagine an idea of the 'good life' that's also an unhappy life. Perhaps we might think that a good life is a life in which we *sacrifice* happiness in this life in favour of a hoped-for life to come. Or we might think that happiness makes us shallow and that if we brood deeply on life, then we'll realize that we *are* not and *cannot* be happy; and that this truth is more important than superficial happiness. Or we might suspect that there are good and noble reasons for us to cultivate not happiness but unhappiness: after all, there are many things that take place in the world that we perhaps should not put up with, and putting happiness above all other values might have all kinds of unwelcome results. So in this third part I hope to raise a number of questions about wider implications of the ways that we think about happiness.

At the end of the book I will make some suggestions for further reading, so that you can explore some of the ideas raised here in more depth. There's a huge and growing body of scholarship on happiness in a wide variety of disciplines, from social science to philosophy, and from psychology to politics. Unfortunately, much of this research is buried in obscure and often expensive journals. Fortunately, there's also a good quantity of thoughtful material written for a more general audience and, as a result, much more easily accessible. I will limit my recommendations to those things that should be easy to track down.

Not a single thing

One thing I will be arguing again and again in this book is that happiness may not turn out to be a single thing, and that there are various kinds of things that we call 'happiness', not all of them mutually compatible. I will also be making the case that happiness is not the only thing that we might hope for or aspire to. Sometimes it's said that there's only one mountain but many roads that lead to the top. However, when it comes to giving shape to our lives, there may be a great many mountains, and the various roads we might tread may lead to very different destinations. Many philosophical approaches to happiness are tied in, either explicitly or implicitly, with the question of what it is that makes a 'good life', but there's no reason to believe that there's only one form of the good life.

 Ideas of happiness are almost always tangled up with ideas about what it is that makes a 'good life'.

This is, when it comes down to it, why claims to have found *the* secret of happiness are suspect; and it's also why you shouldn't expect to find that the ideas in this book all fit together neatly into a whole. But what you *should* find is that, through trying out the various approaches and experiments, you're able to ask some interesting questions about what it means to lead a good and happy life. By the end of this book, you *may* of course be happier. I hope, at least, that you will not be unhappier. But what I hope most of all is this: that you will have a deeper appreciation and understanding of what it means for us to talk about happiness; that you will have a degree of greater scepticism when it comes to those who make claims that they have 'discovered' the secret of happiness; and that you will have a better appreciation of some of the mountainous territory that is the philosophy (and science, and psychology, and economics) of happiness, and how it might be possible to find your way through this territory, so that you're better able to decide where it is that you want to take yourself.

Part I
What is Happiness?

1. The philosophy of happiness

In brief
In the popular imagination, philosophers aren't known to be particularly cheerful individuals. In this chapter we'll explore the long bias in Western philosophy towards gloom, and we'll also ask why a philosophical approach to happiness might nevertheless be useful.

Gloomy philosophers

Several years ago I was talking to a philosopher friend. 'Surely,' I said in the midst of our conversation, 'it's not philosophically more correct to wake up with a heavy heart than it is to wake up full of joy.' My friend paused. 'Perhaps not,' he said, 'but if you want to argue that, you will have most of the Western philosophical tradition against you.'

This isn't entirely true. As we shall see later, there are some philosophers in the West who have escaped this habit of gloom. Nevertheless, it remains the case that Western philosophy seems to have about it a rather gloomy cast of mind. Nobody goes to sit in on a philosophy class because they think it might cheer them up. There's also a broader tendency to equate depth and profundity with gloom, and any kind of optimism or good cheer with shallowness. This seems to me like a mistake. There is such a thing as shallow gloominess, and there is perhaps also such a thing as profound good cheer. Or, to put things differently, there's no clear necessary connection between the emotional tone of one's thinking and its depth.

THINK ABOUT IT
Are sadness and gloom necessarily more profound than happiness? Can you think of any things (books or films, for example) that might support this idea? Can you think of any that are both cheerful *and* profound?

Nevertheless, Western philosophy has tended, for better or worse, to err on the side of gloom. As the philosopher Hegel once said, happiness is simply not the kind of thing that great philosophical minds are given to. In fact, Hegel claimed that although one can survey the history of the world from the point of view of happiness, if one does so, *then the pages are blank*. There is no history of happiness: history itself is a tale of misery and woe and struggle.

KEY FIGURE
Georg Wilhelm Friedrich Hegel (1770–1831) is one of the best-known German philosophers. He's important for his understanding of the relationship between philosophy and history, and his philosophy was a great influence on that of Karl Marx. He wasn't known to be particularly cheerful.

So if we're going to ask about the philosophy of happiness, we need first to ask whether this philosophical bias may have something in it. Perhaps it *is* more philosophically correct to steer clear of happiness. And of all the philosophers in the West, the one who is perhaps most famed for his pessimistic outlook, and who best exemplifies this tendency to equate gloom with philosophical depth, is the German philosopher Schopenhauer, a contemporary of Hegel.

KEY FIGURE Arthur Schopenhauer (1788–1860) taught, like Hegel, at the University of Berlin. Notoriously, he scheduled his lectures at the same time as those of Hegel, but was furious to find that nobody turned up to his own lectures. Schopenhauer is most famous as a philosopher of *pessimism*.

It was Schopenhauer who wrote that 'Everything in life proclaims that earthly happiness is destined to be frustrated or recognized as an illusion. The grounds for this lie deep in the very nature of things.' This is a philosophical claim: there are *reasons* for pessimism, he says, that are rooted in the very nature of things. If we think that we're happy, in other words, then we're simply not thinking hard enough. We're deluded, subject to an illusion. So what reasons does Schopenhauer give to be cheerless?

Reasons to be cheerless

There are essentially two reasons that Schopenhauer gives for his claim that pessimism is the way to go. The first draws on our experience. 'If the immediate and direct purpose of our life is not suffering,' he writes, 'then our existence is the most ill-adapted to its purpose in the world.' For Schopenhauer, we treat every misfortune that befalls us as an exception; but when we look more broadly, we see that misfortune itself is the general rule, even if it comes in many different guises. Pain ultimately outweighs pleasure. Schopenhauer encourages us to try a short thought-experiment to put this claim to the test. The experiment goes something like this:

 Imagine a scene from a wildlife documentary in which a lion is eating an antelope. Try to think your way into the scene to imagine the lion's pleasure and the antelope's suffering, and ask yourself:

- Does the suffering of the antelope outweigh the pleasure of the lion?
- Does this mean that suffering in general outweighs pleasure in general? If so, why? If not, why not?

Now try to find some problems in Schopenhauer's argument by thinking of any situations in which pleasure or happiness manage to outweigh even extreme pain. For example, you might think of somebody who is in considerable pain from an illness, but who claims nevertheless to be happy. Do these act as good arguments against Schopenhauer or not?

For Schopenhauer, if we contemplate the lion and the antelope, we should come to the conclusion that it's absurd to set our sights on happiness, because happiness doesn't go very far at all, while suffering opens up before us like an abyss. We should stop looking for happiness, and set our sights on making the best of the bad job that is living in a world full of suffering.

Philosophical **pessimism** is the idea that there are good reasons to believe that the world is made in such a way that suffering is the general rule.

The second reason Schopenhauer gives for his pessimism is philosophically deeper. Without getting caught up in too many technicalities, we can say that Schopenhauer, like the philosopher Immanuel Kant, and like philosophers in the West ever since the time of ancient Greece, was preoccupied with the gulf between how things actually *are*, and how they *appear* to our perceptions.

Immanuel Kant (1724–1804) lived in Königsberg, now known as Kaliningrad. His work explored not just what we can know about the world, but also the *limits* of our knowledge. He's considered among the greatest philosophers in all of the European tradition.

For Schopenhauer, nature consists of an 'outer' aspect of physical causes and surfaces and also an 'inner' dynamic that he calls the 'Will'. You could see the Will in Schopenhauer's thought as a surging, impersonal force that runs through everything, fashioning us and our desires. How do we know there is such a thing? Because, Schopenhauer says, we have inner, first-person experience of this Will. While we see all other things in terms of their appearances, we experience ourselves *from the inside* as not just a bundle of appearances but an existence that struggles and surges and clings to survival. And if *we* have such an inner dynamic, we can conclude that it's not *just us* (Schopenhauer says that to conclude that only we have this Will is a conclusion that belongs in the madhouse), but that this surge of the Will is the inner dynamic that drives *all things*.

The **Will** in Schopenhauer's philosophy is the name that he gives to an impersonal force that drives all existence. It doesn't belong to us, nor does it have our interests at stake. Which is why, no doubt, we might find ourselves doing stupid things that we later regret, or why we might wake up in the morning to find that we've spent the night with somebody we really shouldn't have done. The Will seeks its own expression, but it doesn't seek our own happiness.

Schopenhauer argues that pessimism is both more rational and more strongly justified by experience. Is he right? If so, why? If not, why not?

The best of a bad job

So there are reasons — at least as far as Schopenhauer is concerned — not to be cheerful. But fortunately Schopenhauer doesn't leave us with nothing other than misery and desolation. Instead he makes some proposals about how we can make the best of the bad job that is our existence, even going so far as to set out some recommendations for how we might lead a more or less 'happy' existence. Schopenhauer himself was aware that this attempt to make life bearable was, philosophically speaking, a compromise; but given his vision of the awfulness of things, such compromises were nevertheless *humanly* necessary. In setting out his philosophy of happiness, Schopenhauer drew in particular upon two traditions that will appear later on in this book: the Buddhism of India, and the thought of the Stoic philosophers of classical Greece and Rome.

For Schopenhauer, the search for happiness was a matter of acting in such a way as to diminish the painfulness of existence. And one way of doing this is by recognizing, to paraphrase him somewhat, that the universe doesn't owe us a happy existence. Here we can see how pessimism may, perhaps somewhat counter-intuitively, be useful in terms of living our lives, as a way of helping us cope with the worst aspects of existence. As far as Schopenhauer is concerned, if we think that the universe is going to provide us with whatever we want, if we think that if only we behave, or if only we live a good enough life, or if only we pray to the right God, then somehow things will go our way, we will in the end find ourselves perpetually disappointed.

For Schopenhauer, recognizing the reality and the inevitability of suffering, although it may not free us from the suffering itself, nevertheless frees us from the hankering that things might be otherwise.

Similarly, when it comes to our dealings with other people, Schopenhauer bluntly says that there are many fools in the world, and fools cause all kinds of misery. But we only add misery to misery if we long for a world in which the fools are no longer fools, in which we wish that those who cause us suffering might somehow be reformed. Schopenhauer's recommendations, in fact, are more or less as follows.

- Firstly, don't seek out happiness but instead seek to diminish your misery.
- Secondly, recognize that the universe is probably never going to deliver us with the happiness we want.
- Thirdly, don't assume that the things that we generally think will make us happy – wealth, power, a new lover – will in fact make us happy: the impersonal Will that surges through us may cause us to desire all kinds of things, but the Will doesn't desire those things that are best for us.

 Schopenhauer doesn't recommend that we try to increase our happiness; but he does recommend that we try to diminish the misery of our lives. But is decreasing our misery the same as increasing our happiness?

Seeking advice on happiness
Nevertheless, it's hard not to think that Schopenhauer wasn't best placed to give advice on happiness, if only because he himself wasn't of a particularly cheery disposition. And

when it comes to *practical* advice, then surely this matters. Listening to Schopenhauer on happiness is like listening to an overweight doctor on the importance of a healthy diet: however good the reasoning, there's something that doesn't quite ring true.

IF YOU REMEMBER ONE THING We need to ask two questions about philosophical pessimism. The first is whether it's *philosophically correct*: has Schopenhauer, in other words, reasoned correctly? The second question is whether it's *humanly useful*: does it actually help us? Some philosophers might claim that these are two very distinct questions, but I'm not so sure. We can't entirely disentangle our reasoning from our ideas and judgements about what it might mean to live well, from our changing emotional states and moods, or from the actual, practical ways that we go about leading our lives.

And if we leave aside for a moment some of Schopenhauer's deeper philosophical claims about the nature of the Will, we can certainly begin to wonder whether his advice is really all there is to be said about human happiness.

2. What we talk about when we talk about happiness

In brief
When philosophers talk about happiness, one of the most important distinctions they make is between what's called a 'hedonic' idea of happiness and a 'eudaimonistic' idea of happiness, between the idea of happiness as pleasure and happiness as flourishing. In this chapter we'll look more closely at this distinction.

Not a single thing?

It was Kant who noted that when you start to think about the problem of happiness from a philosophical viewpoint, things often become rather puzzling. 'The concept of happiness', Kant wrote, 'is such an indeterminate one that even though everyone wishes to attain happiness, yet he can never say definitely and consistently what it is that he really wishes and wills.'

Having already explored a few of the different senses in which we use the word 'happiness', and having looked at Kierkegaard's reflections on marriage and its relation to a happy life, it should be clear that life is messier and more perplexing than most philosophers (who are usually, when it comes down to it, tidy-minded souls) would like. Nevertheless, there's one useful philosophical distinction we can make to help us think through the idea of happiness: that between **hedonic** happiness, or pleasure, and **eudaimonistic** happiness, or flourishing.

Hedonic happiness and the pleasures of life

Perhaps the most straightforward and basic sense of 'happiness' is the one in which we're talking about our immediate experience of what might be called a happy 'feeling'. Philosophers call this *feeling* of happiness 'hedonic' happiness.

Imagine that you win the lottery. You would probably expect to experience a burst of pleasure, even a kind of joy. But research has shown that such bursts of pleasure on the part of lottery-winners are often short-lived. Indeed, what often seems to happen is that, once they win the lottery, people simply adjust their expectations and go back to being more or less as happy as they were before. And this is only to be expected. After all, it would be simply exhausting to be beaming with delight every waking hour.

Hedonic happiness refers to pleasure. The word *hedonic* is related to *hedonism*, and both terms come from the Greek root *hedone*, which simply means 'pleasure'. *Hedone* is linked to *hedys*, which means 'sweet', so you could say that hedonic

24

happiness is the kind of happiness concerned with the sweetness of our experience: the sweetness of lying with a lover, the sweetness of the pleasures of eating and drinking, the delight of meeting up with an old friend.

This kind of happiness is more or less subjective, in that it concerns our own experience of immediate pleasure, and it's also more or less fleeting, in that it doesn't necessarily endure for very long.

Ethics and eudaimonistic happiness

Many of the ancient philosophers, although they were certainly interested in the idea of pleasure, considered that there was a broader sense of the word 'happiness'. And when the famously tormented 20th-century philosopher Ludwig Wittgenstein said on his death-bed, 'Tell them I've had a wonderful life' (the reference to the movie may not be accidental, as Wittgenstein had a weakness for popular films), he probably didn't mean, 'Tell them I've had a life full of pleasure.' Reading Wittgenstein's biography, it's clear that this was not a man who spent his days indulging in merriment. But this death-bed claim makes more sense if we understand it as meaning: 'Tell them I've had a rich, full and meaningful life.' It's perfectly possible that you can have a full, rich and meaningful life, a life that could be called, in one sense, 'happy', without having a life filled with pleasures.

There are perhaps many occasions on which we have the experience of fulfilment without the experience of hedonic pleasure. Human beings being what they are, there's often a kind of strange happiness that comes from difficulty: swimming the Channel, climbing a mountain, reading the complete works of Immanuel Kant in German, or working out how to perform differential calculus. And while doing these things may not provide us with continual bursts of pleasure, as we're slogging our way to the South Pole in sub-zero temperatures, the wind howling about us, our whole body screaming in agony as we take one step after another, we might nevertheless think: 'I could not imagine myself happier than being precisely where I am here and now.'

We need, then, another idea of happiness that doesn't depend on the notion of pleasure. For this we can turn to the philosopher Aristotle (384–322 BCE), who proposed the notion of *eudaimonia*, or 'flourishing'.

KEY TERM

The term **eudaimonia** also comes from the Greek, with *eu* meaning 'well' or 'good', and *daimon* meaning something like 'guiding spirit'. It's often translated as 'flourishing', to distinguish it from hedonic ideas of happiness.

Eudaimonia is sometimes thought of as an **objective**, rather than a **subjective**, account of happiness. In other words, to talk about 'flourishing' suggests that we have an idea of some kind of objective standard against which we can measure the good life.

People find different things pleasurable to different degrees, and the only way to establish what is pleasurable is to ask people: so pleasure is a subjective state. Even if we think that people shouldn't find torturing small animals pleasurable, if the torturer says, 'I experience intense *pleasure* when I hear the critters squeal', then we have to take their word for it. But if somebody says, 'A *flourishing* life is a life in which not a single day goes past without tormenting some small, nervous mammal', then this looks like an objective claim that we can dispute or disagree with.

What this implies is that a eudaimonistic account of happiness is linked to concerns with **ethics**, with questions about what *ought* to be the case for human life, and with questions about *how* we should live our lives.

 Hedonic happiness (pleasure) and eudaimonistic happiness (flourishing) don't always go together. Although there may be occasions when they do coincide, there are other occasions when they are very different things.

Two approaches to happiness

The table on the next page gives us an overview of the distinction between these two approaches to happiness.

Hedonic happiness	Eudaimonistic happiness
• Subjective • Immediate: here and now • Emotional • A matter of personal experience rather than broader moral or political questions	• Objective • Longer term: a whole lifetime? • Evaluative – a matter of evaluating whether we're flourishing • Explicitly concerned with ethics and moral questions

The following exercise is a way of exploring this distinction in more detail.

Visit the website of your favourite newspaper and search for the word 'happiness'. See what articles come up. If there are none, then try a more cheerful newspaper.

Now look in detail at the first five articles and ask:

1. For each reference to 'happiness', in what sense is the word being used? Is the author talking about hedonic or eudaimonistic happiness? Or is there another meaning?
2. For each article, is the idea of happiness consistent throughout, or does it change according to context?
3. Finally, what is the author saying about happiness? Do you agree? If so, why? If not, why not?

Psychologists and social scientists are sometimes cautious of eudaimonistic accounts of happiness, because they see their own role as merely *describing* what is the case. The eudaimonistic approach *prescribes* how we ought to live, and this goes beyond the usual job description of psychologists and social scientists.

Later on in this book we will come to the question of the relationship between thinking about happiness and thinking about ethics, and the impossibility of entirely disentangling the two; but before we do, we should look in more detail at the contemporary approaches to happiness in psychology and the social sciences, and at the idea that there might be such a thing as a 'science' of happiness.

3. A science of happiness?

In brief
If happiness has been one of the central concerns in philosophy since the very beginning, more recently scientists, economists and psychologists have started to explore the idea as well, and have even proposed that we need a 'new science of happiness'. In this chapter, we look more closely at this idea of the science of happiness, and at the movement known as positive psychology.

What is positive psychology?

It's not just philosophers who have tended to be of a gloomy cast of mind. Psychologists have often been no better. For example, early in the 20th century, Sigmund Freud, the father of psychoanalysis, famously said that the purpose of his psychotherapeutic methods was the transformation of hysterical misery into ordinary, everyday unhappiness. And since Freud's day, psychology has spent a great deal of time describing forms of life that have gone awry, cataloguing the varieties of human unhappiness. However, far less attention has been given to those forms of life that have gone right, and the states of mind that might support these forms of life.

In the year 2000, psychologists Martin Seligman and Mihaly Csikszentmihalyi argued that psychology needs to move away from this exclusive focus on all that goes wrong in human life, to chart also the realms of 'positive' experience. Since this call for a new psychology of positive states, experiences and institutions, positive psychology has grown into a vibrant field of study.

Positive psychology is, in the words of positive psychology researchers Jonathan Haidt and Shelly L. Gable, the study of 'the domain of optimal human functioning'.

Positive psychologists aim to redress what they claim is a one-sided approach to psychology by asking if there might be more to human psychology than a catalogue of neuroses and pathologies. The aim of positive psychology is not just to study what makes us *sick of mind*, but also what makes us *healthy of mind*. While psychologists may in the past have dealt with mental disorders of one variety or another, those in the positive psychology movement claim that this is a partial picture unless we study what goes right as well.

This is not to say that positive psychology is necessarily an attempt to ignore the darker side of psychology. Instead, it's an attempt to point out that while there are states of suffering, there are also states of joy, that while there are characters who are lacking empathy, there are also those who are unusually compassionate, and that while human experience has a great many troughs, it also has a great many peaks; and without considering positive experiences such as happiness, a sense of well-being, joy and so forth, psychology is simply incomplete as a descriptive science.

However, as we shall see, positive psychology's aims are not just descriptive. As Seligman and Csikszentmihalyi make clear, their aim is to understand not just 'what *is*' but also 'what *could be*'.

Philosophers and psychologists

Let's look more closely at this question of 'what could be'. If we go back to Haidt and Gable's idea of 'optimal human functioning', we find ourselves having to ask what we mean by 'optimal'. Optimal, in other words, for what? Seligman and Csikszentmihalyi make some attempt to answer this question, saying that positive psychology is about those virtues that lead to 'better citizenship; responsibility, nurturance, altruism, civility, moderation, tolerance, and work ethic'. However, as we shall discover later, there are philosophical approaches to happiness that are neither particularly civil, nor marked by a strong work ethic. There are perspectives from which a work ethic seems sub-optimal, while lounging around in the sun without any higher purpose seems about as optimal as it gets.

Seligman writes that positive psychology has three purposes: firstly, to study positive emotions; secondly, to study positive traits such as virtues and character strengths; and thirdly, to study positive institutions. Before going on, it might be worth stopping to make some notes on your own thoughts and ideas about what these things might be.

Take a sheet of paper and divide it into three columns as below. Now list as many positive emotions, character strengths and virtues, and positive institutions as you can think of.

Positive emotions	Character strengths and virtues	Positive institutions

If you want to take this experiment further, get a friend to do the same thing. When you've finished your lists, compare notes with each other and see if you agree. Where do you disagree, and why? On what basis did you make your decision about what was a positive emotion, a strength, a virtue or a positive institution?

Now have a look at this list compiled from some of the literature on positive psychology:

Positive emotions	Character strengths and virtues	Positive institutions
Well-being	Capacity for love	Democracy
Contentment	Courage	Strong families
Hope	Interpersonal skills	Free inquiry
Optimism	Forgiveness	
'Flow'	Originality	
Happiness	Spirituality	

Finally, ask yourself where you agree with this list, and where you disagree.

This should raise some interesting questions. Imagine, for example, that Joe believes strong families are positive institutions, while Josie believes the exemplary social unit is the anarchist squat; or imagine that Betty believes optimism is really for the best, while Bertrand, who has been reading Schopenhauer, believes pessimism is the better option.

Part of the problem here is that it's not clear how we should decide what a positive emotion, or a virtue, or a positive institution *is*. Some emotions, for example pride, are considered strongly positive in some contexts, and strongly negative in other contexts. Is it always the case that families and democracies are by their very natures positive institutions? History shows that many families, and many democracies, are implicated in some of the worst forms of human behaviour.

And so one problem that positive psychology faces is that it can't avoid a deeper philosophical questioning of what the good life actually is. This isn't just an issue with *positive* psychology, but with psychology more generally: the approach to psychology that diagnoses disorders also has to settle, explicitly or implicitly, on an idea of the good life, to the extent that those it treats depart from this norm. When it comes to ideas of the good life, in short, there's no escaping philosophy.

Whenever we talk about 'positive emotions', 'virtues' or 'positive institutions', we're already making philosophical claims about what makes a 'good' life.

The science and politics of happiness

In the realm of physics, we've made considerable advances from the time of the ancient Greeks. No amount of reading

Aristotle's *Physics* will allow you to design an aircraft that actually flies. Modern physics, in other words, has far outstripped the physics of the ancients: the scientists have moved in and the philosophers have moved out. When it comes to the science of happiness, some positive psychologists suggest that the same might happen – that positive psychology might provide us with a way of deciding once and for all between the different approaches to happiness in the history of philosophy, to ask which of the philosophers got happiness 'right'.

But is this true? If our science of happiness is already tangled up in value judgements about happiness and the good life, then it's unlikely that this new science, if indeed it is a science, will be able to do away with philosophy any time soon.

We have already seen that if we don't take account of what we might call 'positive' states then, as a descriptive science, psychology is incomplete. But this aim at a more complete descriptive psychology isn't quite the same thing as a science of happiness. And it's clear that for some positive psychologists the aims of positive psychology go far beyond this idea of a descriptive science. Indeed, when positive psychologists talk about exploring not only what 'is' but what 'could be', then they're being frank in their admission of this fact.

However, the current interest in positive psychology isn't just restricted to psychologists or those who read popular psychology books because they would like to be a little happier. There's also a growing interest in positive psychology on the part of governments, businesses and other organizations. Positive psychology, in other words, has become a broader political issue. But if we want to maintain a broader political vision of what 'could be', we might want to resist any tendencies to take too narrow a view of happiness.

Happiness is not just a personal issue. The question of what the 'good life' involves is also a **political** question.

When you look at the various philosophical approaches to happiness, it's hard not to conclude that philosophers are, in general, an unruly bunch. And while some philosophical notions of happiness dovetail well with those of the positive psychologists, others seem to suggest very different visions of the good life. The danger is that, in its enthusiasm for the idea of a 'science of happiness', positive psychology, for all its usefulness, might tend to tame and perhaps to diminish the somewhat unruly notion of happiness, and might therefore limit our vision of the possible forms of the good life. We will return to these questions at the end of this book.

4. Calculating happiness

In brief

Here we turn to an idea that goes back to the philosopher Jeremy Bentham: the idea that happiness can be measured. In this chapter we'll look at Bentham's attempts to measure happiness, and at the idea of 'subjective well-being' in positive psychology. We'll also explore some of the philosophical questions around the idea of measuring happiness.

Two sovereign masters

One of the central ideas of positive psychology is that happiness is a quantity that may be measured. To look at this, it will help to go back to the philosopher Jeremy Bentham. In the late 18th and early 19th centuries, Bentham was one of the first thinkers to try to put happiness on a scientific, which is to say a *measurable*, footing.

KEY FIGURE   Jeremy Bentham (1748–1832) was an English lawyer and philosopher, and the founder of the philosophical movement known as 'Utilitarianism'. Though trained in the law, he became disillusioned with the irrational, chaotic and arbitrary state of legislation. Law seemed the antithesis of a rigorous science, without any clear principles, a huge mass of exceptions and precedents and faulty reasoning. Bentham dreamed of putting law on a firm and unambiguous footing, not only so that we might be able to distinguish the good from the bad, but also so that we might be able to say precisely *how* good or bad something was. Thanks to the rather peculiar terms of his will, Bentham bequeathed his body to University College London, where it still sits in embalmed form.

Bentham started from two very fundamental aspects of our experience, what he called the 'two sovereign masters': *pain* and *pleasure*. They are 'masters' because they guide our actions: we act to maximize pleasure and to diminish pain. Bentham realized that, if this was the case, then if we want to know how we *should* act, and how we should pass judgement on the actions of others, we simply need to work out which actions lead to the greatest maximizing of pleasure and the greatest reduction of pain.

For Bentham, this isn't just about *my own* pleasure and pain, but about a broader social vision: in calculating which actions best maximize pleasure and minimize pain, I have to factor in the broadest possible range of outcomes of my action. Perhaps I get some pleasure from hitting you over the head with a rock, but if we factor in the discomfort that you feel, then it becomes clear that I should probably refrain. And if I get pleasure from hitting you over the head with a cat, then we have to consider the cat in the calculations as well.

For Bentham, there are several factors we need to consider in calculating the consequences of an action in terms of pleasure and pain.

- We need to think about the *intensity* of pleasure or pain, the question of how much.
- We also need to think about the *duration*, the question of how long. After all, we might prefer a brief second of serious pain to a year of nagging suffering.
- Then there's *certainty*, or how likely it is that this action will lead to pleasure or pain.
- There's also *propinquity*, how near-at-hand the pain or pleasure is going to be – for example, we might think something is worth doing for a small increase in pleasure tomorrow, but if this small increase in pleasure is in ten years' time, it might be less worthwhile.
- Then there's the question of *fecundity*, or how likely this pleasure or pain is to give rise to more of the same.
- And finally, there's *purity*, or whether the pain or the pleasure is likely to turn into or to entail the opposite, just as the pleasure of drinking a bottle of wine can entail the discomfort of a hangover the following day.

In this exercise, we'll try out Bentham's 'Hedonic Calculus'. Think of a decision that you need to make, but that you're not sure about. Now fill in the following two charts by ticking the relevant boxes, first for the likely outcomes in terms of pleasure, and then for the likely outcomes in terms of pain.

Pleasure

	High	Medium	Low
Intensity			
Duration			
Certainty			
Propinquity			
Fecundity			
Purity			

Pain

	High	Medium	Low
Intensity			
Duration			
Certainty			
Propinquity			
Fecundity			
Purity			

You'll also need to think about the number of people (or other sentient creatures) implicated in your decision. So if there are 100 people for whom it might lead to undesirable outcomes, this might outweigh the ten people for whom this might lead to desirable outcomes.

After filling in the charts as best you can, ask yourself whether you can make your decision based on these likely outcomes of pleasure and pain.

The problem here is immediately clear: *how do we actually perform the necessary calculations?* What units do we use to measure pleasure? And pain? And how do we know that we have sufficient data? After all, we need to consider all possible implications of any action, and if we're going to perform actual calculations, we have to do this with a degree of rigour. This approach to deciding the right thing to do might work as a rule of thumb, but when it comes to putting it on firmer foundations, it becomes much more difficult to see how we should make these decisions.

But the idea of happiness as a measurable quantity hasn't gone away. More recently with positive psychology, it has returned in the form of the idea of 'subjective well-being'.

Subjective well-being

In all but the most limited approaches to happiness, it seems clear that we're not just talking about mapping our fleeting experiences of pleasure. Any substantial notion of happiness needs to include some idea of *how well our life is going*. If you've ever been involved in a psychological survey about your life, you may have been asked questions like: 'How happy are you with the way your life is going?'; or 'Are you satisfied with your life?' These are clearly not only

43

questions about the amount of pleasure that you experience, but also take into account broader considerations relating to how well you're faring. It's perfectly possible to experience a great many pleasures, and at the same time to think that life isn't really going well for us. And it's perfectly possible to have the sense that life is going well for us, but to experience little in the way of subjective pleasure.

The notion of subjective well-being (sometimes written simply as SWB) is a way of trying to get at some hard, objective data on what seems most subjective: our own sense of how life is going for us. It does this by relying on the *reportability* of subjective states, the fact that I can say that yesterday things were going well for me, and that today things are going less well for me. So while how you feel may be *subjective*, your report about how you're feeling turns this kind of first-person experience into *objective* third-person data. Subjective well-being research relies on questionnaires and surveys that require the participants to respond to questions related to their own evaluations of their lives.

 This can most easily be made clear by means of an example. The five statements below come from the Satisfaction With Life Scale (SWLS), developed by researchers Ed Diener, Robert Emmons, Randy Larsen and Sharon Griffin. For each statement, give yourself a mark from 1 to 7 where 1 is 'strongly disagree', 4 is 'neither agree nor disagree' and 7 is 'strongly agree'. Then add up the figures to give yourself a total.

The Satisfaction With Life Scale

_____ In most ways my life is close to my ideal.

_____ The conditions of my life are excellent.

_____ I am satisfied with my life.

_____ So far I have got the important things I want in life.

_____ If I could live my life over, I would change almost nothing.

_____ **TOTAL**

Your total should be between 5 and 35. The scores break down into broad bands as follows:

31–35	Extremely satisfied
26–30	Satisfied
21–25	Slightly satisfied
20	Neutral
1–19	Slightly dissatisfied
10–14	Dissatisfied
5–9	Extremely dissatisfied

You may want to take this short test every day for a week, to chart the comings and goings of your subjective well-being.

It may be that on Monday you're more or less happy (total of 27), on Tuesday you lose your job (total of 13), then on Wednesday, because you're not at work, you go to the park and promptly fall in love (your total goes up to 32), but then on Thursday you realize that the person you've fallen in love with is leaving for Panama the coming weekend (the score plummets to 5). In this fashion we can track changes in our well-being.

If you're a philosopher, and therefore awkward, you may find that this approach to happiness raises a few problems. Perhaps you don't have an 'ideal' with which you compare your life. Perhaps you have the sense that getting the important things you want isn't as important as all that. Perhaps you're puzzled by which of the things you want are important and which aren't. Or perhaps you're mystified by the final question about living your life over. What does this mean? What are you permitted to change in this thought-experiment: just your own decisions, or do you have discretion when it comes to the laws of physics?

So now, looking back over the list of statements from the Satisfaction With Life Scale, have a think about the following questions.

 Do the answers you've given on the subjective well-being scale really reflect your life satisfaction? And do they really reflect your

46

happiness (which may or may not be the same thing)? What kind of assumptions about the nature of happiness do you think there might be in the Satisfaction With Life Scale?

Questions about subjective well-being

Although at first glance the idea of subjective well-being may seem to be close to a eudaimonistic notion of happiness, there's an important difference. Subjective well-being is an evaluation of how life is going for *me*, but philosophers of eudaimonistic happiness often make broader claims about what it is that makes a good life. It would be perfectly possible, within a eudaimonistic theory of happiness, to say that somebody had 'lived a happy life', even if they didn't report any level of subjective well-being.

Flora was a novelist. Her books were unpublished during her lifetime but were discovered posthumously and are now considered to be classics of literature.

Throughout her life, Flora was troubled by self-doubt. In fact, one day a psychologist knocked on her door and asked: 'Are you satisfied with your life?' Flora howled: 'No! How can I be satisfied? Nobody reads the words that I labour over day and night!' The psychologist apologized and moved on down the street.

Flora, in other words, experienced almost no subjective well-being. But once her books were published, a literary critic wrote in the newspaper that her books were 'a testament to a rich and flourishing inner life'.

Was Flora happy or not? Was the critic wrong? Is it possible that the critic was right, even if Flora experienced *no* subjective well-being?

For all of its problems, subjective well-being is a useful measure precisely because it's something measurable. Through studies of subjective well-being we know, for example, that while being poor correlates with lack of well-being, as you become richer, in terms of subjective well-being you become subject to the law of diminishing returns: doubling your income if you're on the breadline will make a big difference to your life; doubling your income if you're super-rich will have a negligible effect. These kinds of measure can be used to explore the gains and losses in well-being of everything from marriage to death of a spouse, to losing one's job, to child-rearing (incidentally, and perhaps contrary to expectations, it seems to be fairly well established that having children correlates with a somewhat lower level of overall life satisfaction).

In other words, if we want our theory of happiness to provide us with more or less objective measures, then subjective well-being may be the way to go; but there are other kinds of questions we can ask about happiness, questions that go beyond ideas of pleasure and of subjective well-being. We will explore some of these questions in the next chapter.

5. Happiness and ethics

In brief
Most philosophies of happiness in the ancient and medieval worlds were less concerned with the problem of 'measuring' happiness than with the connection between happiness and the way we lead our lives. For many such philosophers, the happy life and the good life go together. In other words, if we're asking about happiness, we're also asking about ethics.

What do we want from a theory of happiness?
The approach that we take to the question of happiness will depend, in large part, on what we want our theory of happiness to *do*.

For example, if we're interested in formulating public policy, the idea of subjective well-being may be a useful one. It can be useful to know that low subjective well-being is often correlated with high crime rates and that high subjective well-being correlates positively with availability of public parks and green spaces. This information might suggest that one thing we could do to tackle crime is not to make the justice system more punitive, but rather to make cities greener and more pleasant to live in. Similarly, we might look at the strong evidence that extensive advertising to children correlates with low levels of subjective well-being; and seeing this, we might be persuaded to limit the powers of businesses that advertise directly to the very young. Or we might take the evidence that happiness tends to decrease the wider the gulf becomes between the very richest and the very poorest, and use this as a justification for addressing some of the inequities within society. All of these steps might well be of wider public benefit.

But what if we're not just concerned with public policy, but also with the existential question, *How should I live my life?* Here we might find a subjective well-being approach to happiness limiting, and want to take a more eudaimonistic approach, one that allows us to ask: *What kind of life will allow me to flourish the most?* In other words, we might be concerned not just with the *experience* of well-being but also with the *way* in which we're going about living our life.

Finding an ethos

The idea of eudaimonia, in focusing not just on what we experience but also on the question of how we lead our lives, draws an explicit connection between happiness and ethics. This connection between happiness and ethics would have been widely accepted in the ancient world. If happiness is, in the eudaimonistic sense, about what might make my life go better for me, then this will require that I come to some kind of decision about what it means for a life as a whole to go well.

 Like happiness, 'ethics' can mean several things. Sometimes philosophers talk about **normative ethics**, which means thinking about the general principles that might determine whether something is right or wrong. Sometimes they're interested in **applied ethics**, or the application of ethical thinking to tricky situations. There's also a field called **meta-ethics**, in which philosophers attempt to ask bigger questions about what ethics actually is, and try to understand the nature of ethical language.

But the various thinkers we will be exploring later in this book, from Confucius to Aristotle and from Śāntideva to Epicurus, are often concerned with something that isn't really captured by any of these categories, and that's what might be called ethics as *ethos*. Ethics in this sense isn't simply about deciding what's right and what's wrong, or asking how we make such decisions, but about actually *making efforts to live differently*, or to *give a particular shape and form to our lives*. The central question of ethics in this sense is not so much what I should or shouldn't do, but instead the question of what it might mean to live a flourishing life.

REMEMBER THIS!!!

Ethics as *ethos* isn't about deciding what we think is good, right or desirable. Instead it requires what might be called *experiments in living*, an ability to ask: 'What if I were to live otherwise?'

Many of the philosophers we will be looking at in the next part of this book make very strong recommendations about how we might best live otherwise. And many of them share the idea that this attempt to find a way of living is a matter of *practice*. It's not something that we can just do once and for all, still less is it something we can just theorize about; instead it's something in which we must train ourselves.

Experiments in living

These days, if you meet a philosopher, you might ask them what theory they subscribe to, or what philosophical problems they're working on, and they will happily tell you. But you wouldn't think to ask them what they had for breakfast, what kind of bed they slept in, who (if anyone) shared that bed, how they made a living, and what posture they adopted for the purposes of thinking. In fact, these questions would seem decidedly peculiar, if not downright rude. However, in the ancient world, if you happened to stumble across a philosopher, while you would certainly be interested in their ideas, you would also be interested in asking *what they did*. In ancient Greece, in classical China, and in the India of the Buddha's time, it was possible to find a great many people who attempted to explore ethics not just by talking about right and wrong, but by conducting various experiments in living and by attempting to cultivate a particular kind of *ethos*.

It's this experimental openness to various kinds of *ethos* that I want to encourage you to try out in your own explorations of the philosophy of happiness. However, there's a warning here: some of these experiments take long practice; and perhaps only at the end of this long practice will you be able to truly evaluate these recommendations. So this book will give you no more than a taste of some of the possibilities.

Eudaimonia and the paradox of hedonism

Even if a eudaimonistic approach to happiness is a problem for many researchers who don't want to be seen as prescribing or stepping beyond their bounds to suggest how others ought to live, it may nevertheless be useful if you want not just to know about happiness, but actually to be a little bit happier. One reason for this may lie in what's known as the 'hedonic paradox'. This paradox is associated with the 19th-century British philosopher Henry Sidgwick (1838–1900), who made the observation that we can't attain to happiness by aiming at happiness.

The **hedonic paradox** or **paradox of hedonism** is the idea that happiness can't be attained directly, but is instead a side-effect of the choices that we make. Happiness, in other words, isn't something that we can set as a goal within life, but is a side-effect of how we go about the business of living.

Around the same time as Sidgwick, another 19th-century philosopher, John Stuart Mill, wrote in a famous passage in his autobiography:

> I never, indeed, wavered in the conviction that happiness is the test of all rules of conduct, and the end of life. But I now thought that this end was only to be attained by not making it the direct end. Those only are happy (I thought) who have their minds fixed on some object other than their own happiness; on the happiness of others, on the improvement of mankind, even on some art or pursuit, followed not as a means, but as itself an ideal end. Aiming thus at something else, they find happiness by the way.

KEY FIGURE John Stuart Mill (1806–73) was a philosopher who developed Bentham's 'Utilitarian' approach to questions of happiness and ethics, and who also wrote extensively on politics.

THINK ABOUT IT Can you think of one example of a time in your own life when aiming at happiness was the thing that got in the way of happiness? Can you think of a time when happiness seemed like a side-effect of aiming at something else? What does this say about the paradox of hedonism?

The accordion: a shortcut to happiness?

To explore this paradox a little more, we can have a look at the following case study.

CASE STUDY One day, James read a research paper about the happiness of accordion players. The author of the paper claimed that accordion players were 50 per cent happier than the rest of the population. As it happened, James was feeling down in the dumps, so he went out, bought an accordion and started to learn to play. Days turned to weeks, and weeks to months. The accordion, James discovered, was difficult, far more difficult than he had anticipated. But he persisted with his scales and exercises.

After a year, James realized that he wasn't getting any happier. In fact, with every day that passed, he was becoming less and less happy. He was frustrated with the accordion, frustrated by his slow progress, and found himself wondering whether he even *liked* accordion music.

So: was James's accordion faulty? Or was the research wrong?

The sad case of James and the accordion points us to the problem. It may indeed be true that accordionists are uncommonly cheerful, but this is not because of the magical power that accordions may have to confer happiness upon those who play them. Instead, this happiness is, in Mill's words, a side-effect of the 'art or pursuit, followed not as a means, but as itself an ideal end'. If it's true that accordion players (with the exception of James) are happier than non-accordion players, then it's probably simply because playing the accordion *is what they want to be doing*. The best reason for learning the accordion, in other words, is because you love the accordion, because your conception of the good life is one that involves accordion-playing, and not because you want to be happy. Setting our sights on happiness, if the paradox of hedonism is indeed correct, may be the very thing that gets in the way of the happiness we so strongly desire.

Part II
What Makes Us Happy?

6. Some approaches to happiness

In brief
Happiness has been a central preoccupation of philosophy from the very beginning, not only in the West but also in India, China and further afield. Many philosophers asking about happiness have not been content only to theorize, but have also explored various experiments in living to put their ideas into practice.

In the next section of the book, we'll explore a number of practical approaches to happiness. I don't guarantee that all of them will actually have the effect of making you happier. In fact, I don't guarantee that *any* of them will do so. But taken together, these approaches to happiness make up some of the most interesting answers that have been given to questions like *What is happiness?* and *How can we lead happier lives?*

In the chapters that follow, while I will draw upon philosophers familiar from the Western tradition, I will also explore other ways of thinking about happiness from traditions outside European thought, in particular Buddhist ideas, and ideas from China. Different philosophical traditions have very different preoccupations, and so by exploring a range of these, we can call into question some of the cultural assumptions that we have inherited from our own tradition.

THINK ABOUT IT

Some aspects of happiness itself may in fact be *determined* by culture. What's meant by happiness in Britain, for example, may not be quite the same as what's meant by happiness in China. One interesting case is the question of whether happiness and sadness are mutually exclusive. It's generally considered in the West that they are. For example, in his book on happiness, the economist Richard Layard says that happiness and sadness exist on a scale: the happier we are, the less sad we are, and vice versa. This is, of course, useful to those who want to try to measure happiness on a tidy sliding scale. But although this view of happiness seems to be the norm in the West, there's evidence that 'dialectical emotions', emotions that can be *both* positive and negative, are much more common in East Asia. This kind of cultural difference has implications for how we think about happiness *in general*.

My aim in these chapters is not to provide a coherent view of how we might go about leading happier lives, but rather to explore some of the diversity of the answers that have been given to the question of what it is to live happily and well. And, for each of the approaches that follows, I have set out some practical exercises so that you can not just *think about* the questions raised by these different traditions, but also *do something about* them.

7. Aristotle: excellence, flourishing and virtue

In brief
It was Aristotle who first explored the idea of eudaimonia or 'flourishing'. In this chapter we look in more detail at the idea of flourishing and explore its implications for how we think about happiness today.

When it comes to ideas of happiness in the West, one of the most important and influential figures is the Greek philosopher Aristotle. Aristotle's thinking was so broad and wide-ranging – encompassing logic, biology, statecraft and politics, physics, ethics, literary theory, history, metaphysics and numerous other topics – that in the Middle Ages in Europe he was simply referred to as 'the Philosopher': there was no need to ask which one. And even today, his writings on ethics still inform contemporary debates around happiness.

KEY FIGURE Aristotle was born in the town of Stagira in 384 BCE. His father was physician to the Macedonian court. At the age of seventeen, Aristotle travelled to Athens where he entered Plato's Academy. When Plato died in 367 BCE, Aristotle left Athens and spent the next few years in Assos and Lesbos. It was while he was in Lesbos that he was summoned by Philip of Macedonia to become tutor to his son, Alexander, who later became Alexander the Great. After two years in Macedonia, he returned to Athens and set up his own philosophical school, known as the Lyceum. In Macedonia Alexander succeeded his father Philip and set about his short-lived campaign of conquest of the known world, his ambitions taking him as far east as the Indus river; but after Alexander's death in 323, anti-Macedonian feeling led Aristotle to leave Athens. He died the following year in the city of Chalcis.

Aristotle on happiness

What does Aristotle say about happiness? Let's start with the seemingly uncontroversial idea that happiness is a *good thing*. If we do think of happiness as a good thing, then it might seem that there are many good things for which we might aim, and that happiness is one good thing among many; but Aristotle claims that this isn't quite true. Most of these things we aim at, Aristotle points out, we aim at *for the sake of something else*.

So, for example, imagine that you want to become the chief executive of a large company. Why would you ever want to do such a bizarre thing? Because (Aristotle might say) you want wealth and power. But why do you want wealth and power? Because you might want to live in an enormous mansion, waited on by servants day and night. And why would this be desirable? Because, if you managed to live in this way, you might be happy. But – and this question is the clincher – why do you want to be happy? Well, to paraphrase Aristotle, you just *do*. In other words, there are many things that we might consider 'good' that we desire because they might lead to *something else*, but happiness is a thing that is good *in and of itself*. So happiness, Aristotle says, 'standing by itself alone renders life desirable and lacking in nothing'.

 Try putting this to the test. Note down something that you desire. Now ask yourself: do I want this thing for its own sake, or do I want it because it will help me fulfil some further desire? For example, you might want to learn Ancient Greek. But why? Perhaps you want to learn to read Aristotle in the original language. If you find a further desire such as this, write it down.

Now ask yourself why you want this next thing that you've written down. What further desire is there? Perhaps you want to read Aristotle in the original so that you can become wise. Keep going with this process until you can find no further desires. Your list might look something like this:

- I want to learn to read Ancient Greek.

- BECAUSE I want to read Aristotle in the original language.
- BECAUSE I want to become wise.
- BECAUSE I want to stop doing foolish things that cause me all kinds of trouble.
- BECAUSE I want to be happy.
- BECAUSE ... well, because I want to be happy!

In your own list, do you find yourself ending up with happiness as a final end? Or are other final ends possible?

For Aristotle, happiness is the thing that we desire for its own sake. And by happiness, Aristotle means eudaimonia or flourishing. But what, more precisely, does it mean to flourish? Let's look at how Aristotle sets about answering this question.

In his *Nicomachean Ethics*, Aristotle says that flourishing concerns the 'function' or purpose of human life. Here he invokes the term 'excellence' or *arete*, more often translated as 'virtue'. For Aristotle, excellence can be applied to anything. So, for example, I might have several pens with which to write, but one has ink that continually dries up, one is uncomfortable to hold, and another writes in glitter ink that's distracting when it comes to doing serious philosophy. But when it comes to putting thoughts about Aristotle down on paper, my fountain pen seems to exhibit excellence. Similarly, for Aristotle, things like knives and racehorses can be excellent. What makes a thing excellent is its ability to do well that which it is *for*. Racehorses that race well, pens that write well, knives that cut well, cakes that taste good: these are all examples of excellence or of virtue.

This raises a tricky question. If human virtue is doing well that which we are for, if it's a matter of fulfilling the purpose of human existence, then what is this purpose? Aristotle answers this by asking what makes human beings distinct from other things. And, being a philosopher, he says that what makes us different is *reason*. Reason, for Aristotle, is the faculty we have that no other creatures do, it's the particular excellence of being a human being; and so virtue is a matter of acting in a fashion that expresses reason. It's important to note that reason here isn't just a matter of *sitting and thinking*, but also of how we choose to act. It's this – practical action born out of reason – that constitutes virtue, and that leads to a flourishing or a happy life.

For Aristotle a flourishing life is a life of excellence or virtue (*arete*). As we're distinct from other kinds of things, in that we have the power of reason, virtue implies acting in accord with reason.

Getting lucky

If for Aristotle it's not possible to lead a truly happy life without virtue, when it comes to the question of whether all virtuous lives are necessarily happy lives, the picture becomes more complex. The problem we have is that of the role of luck within a happy life. Surely, after all, there's a measure of luck to our own happiness? You happen to stumble into the right job, or the right relationship, or to be born in the right part of the world, or to have the right set of genes, and all of these things may predispose you to happiness. Indeed, the term eudaimonia has the sense of good fortune, with *daimon* also having the meaning 'luck'. Aristotle himself is aware that this is a potential problem, and he explores it in the *Nicomachean Ethics*, taking as an example Priam, the king of Troy.

CASE STUDY Priam was king of Troy at the time of the Trojan war. According to Aristotle, he was virtuous but also profoundly unlucky: he witnessed the killing of his sons and the fall of his city before he was himself killed by Neoptolemus, the son of Achilles. Priam, in other words, was a model of virtue; but, at least in his final days, he could not be considered to have been happy.

Priam's unlucky ending presents us with a disturbing thought: that there may be limits to what we can do to secure our own happiness. If we don't have control over our fates, then the *possibility* of some kind of calamity or disaster is something that we can't escape. Should this possibility cast a shadow upon our potential for happiness?

The example of Priam is interesting because much contemporary writing on happiness, even some of the writing that draws explicitly on Aristotle, can seem to imply that happiness is *entirely our own affair*, something that depends fundamentally on our own internal capacity for happiness, regardless of external circumstances, as if all we need to do is cultivate virtues such as 'resilience' as a response to misfortune, and we'll be able to rise above anything life throws at us. But at the same time, when your city is destroyed and your children are put to the sword, it's a harsh doctrine that suggests that, if you're left somewhat unhappy with the hand that fate has dealt you, then this is a matter of your lack of resilience, your weakness of character.

 THINK ABOUT IT Think of a time when you were particularly happy. How much of this happiness was down to luck? Do you think that luck is an *inherent* part of happiness? Do you think it's possible to be virtuous but, thanks to bad luck, to also be unhappy?

Living virtuously

Nevertheless, even if we can't guarantee good fortune, it remains the case, as far as Aristotle is concerned, that the most excellent and flourishing life is one of virtue. Aristotle himself notes that happiness may be divine and sent by heaven, or may be won by virtue; but if we can have little power over the fortune that heaven sends, we can at least practise virtue.

This raises the question of what we mean by virtue. In answering this question, Aristotle starts by asking about what we call, in an ordinary, everyday sense, virtuous. Generally, he concludes, we tend to regard the two poles of **excess** or **deficiency** as examples of lack of virtue. We might criticize somebody for being over-friendly or for being stand-offish, for being cowardly or rash, for being too self-effacing or too self-aggrandizing. What we find commendable is the *appropriate* amount of self-effacement, or friendliness, or courage.

 What's important is that this appropriate amount depends on **context**. It's not that there's a perfect amount of friendliness to display in *all* contexts: there's a certain amount of friendliness that's appropriate to *each* context.

For each situation, having neither excess nor deficiency, but instead regulating our actions by means of reason, we attain to the *mean* position ('mean' as in mathematical mean, rather than as in the opposite of 'generous'), in which our actions are neither excessive nor lacking.

The **mean** for Aristotle is the middle state between extremes of action. This is less a question of finding a mid-point on an abstract scale, and more a matter of finding the *appropriate level* of something. So, for example, when it comes to anger, the mean isn't just a matter of being neither lacking in spirit nor harsh-tempered, but also of knowing when and how much anger is appropriate, in response to whom and to which particular situations.

To practise virtue, in other words, we must remain attentive to particular circumstances, using our reason to understand how we might best navigate through them; and because this kind of practical wisdom depends on attention to individual circumstances, it needs to be learned on the job. There's no rule book for practical wisdom. Instead, it's a matter of the accumulation of lifelong experience, of paying attention to the examples of those wiser and more virtuous than ourselves, and of understanding what any set of circumstances might call for.

Hitting the mean

We can explore the idea of the mean in relation to a range of different areas of activity or experience. In the *Nicomachean Ethics*, Aristotle sets out some examples of how the idea of the mean might work in relation to various domains of human life. The chart below gives a summary.

Sphere of activity or experience	Excess	Mean	Deficiency
Dealing with money	Prodigality	Liberality	Stinginess
Dealing with anger	Harsh-temperedness	Feeling anger 'on the right grounds, against the right persons, in the right manner and at the right moment'	Lack of spirit
Dealing with conversation	Buffoonery	Wit	Boorishness
Dealing with others	Obsequious-ness	Friendliness	Cantankerous-ness
Dealing with fear	Rashness	Courage	Cowardice
Dealing with pleasure	Licentiousness	Temperance	Insensibility

With the help of this chart, we can try an exercise to see if we can cultivate Aristotelian virtue and excellence, and thus – if we're lucky and don't fall like Priam into any great misfortune – attain happiness.

Taking the table above as a guide, designate a day in your week to be an 'Aristotle day'. At the end of it, go over the events of the day and ask yourself the extent to which you have managed, or failed, to attain the mean in the various areas of activity you've been involved in. Or, if you want to really test yourself (and you're sure you aren't going to fall out), get a friend to fill it in for you.

If you do this over several days, you should be able to see patterns emerging. The point, for a follower of Aristotle, is to allow this information to inform your conduct in future. Hitting the mean is not so much like an arrow hitting a target – it's more a question of building up a broader and deeper knowledge of how we act in various situations, so that we can begin to change our actions.

Happiness, but not as we know it

At this point you might be asking, haven't we strayed a little way from the idea of happiness? The answer to this must be 'yes and no'. Although for Aristotle a happy life is a life of virtue, a life in which we guide our actions by practical wisdom, a life in which our every action reflects the excellence of living according to the mean, this conception of happiness is very different from what we might have in mind when we complain: 'But all I want is to be happy.' This excellence doesn't amount to a life of happy *feelings*; and if it amounts to a life of subjective well-being, this well-being will be rooted not in any kind of evaluation of how our life is going for us, but in a rational sense that we're living as well as we can, whatever our external circumstances. For Aristotle, the ultimate question is not 'Are you happy with your life?', or 'Are you happy with how life is going for you?', but instead: 'Are you happy with how you have *lived*?'

8. Epicurus: a small pot of cheese

In brief
If Aristotle is the champion of eudaimonistic approaches to happiness in the ancient world, when it comes to hedonic ideas of happiness, we need to turn to Epicurus. But in doing so, we will find that the boundaries between hedonic and eudaimonistic approaches become blurred.

It's fair to say that Epicureanism, named after its founder Epicurus (341–270 BCE), is a philosophical school that has historically had something of a bad press. To say that somebody is an Epicurean is to suggest that they're overly fond of food, drink and other forms of sensual enjoyment; and for much of history the term 'Epicurean' has been associated with luxury and excess. But when we look at Epicurus himself, we find a philosopher who seems a long way from this kind of indulgence in sensual pleasures. 'Send me a small pot of cheese, so that I may be able to indulge myself whenever I wish', Epicurus once wrote to a friend, a sentiment that suggests he has some way to go before he matches the hedonistic excesses of certain rock stars.

Epicureanism is one of the several philosophies of happiness that flourished around the fourth century BCE and that continued to do so for several hundred years in the Greek and Roman worlds. The Epicureans were interested in pleasure (their critics were right on this front), but what they said about pleasure was more subtle than is sometimes imagined. When they talked about happiness, they weren't talking just about pleasure, but about a state that they called *ataraxia*, or 'freedom from disturbance'. This freedom from disturbance was, for Epicurus, the final goal of philosophy and indeed of all knowledge. Epicurus' philosophy, in other words, was first and foremost about ethics, about shaping one's life to support this state of ataraxia. Although Epicurus is interested in other things – for example, physics, or questions about the nature of knowledge (what philosophers call 'epistemology') – he is interested in these insofar as they can contribute to ethics; insofar as they matter for *how we live*.

KEY TERM

Ataraxia, or 'freedom from disturbance', was the ultimate aim of the Epicurean philosophy of happiness.

So, for example, in a letter to one of his followers, Epicurus recommends studying astronomy; not because he thinks that a knowledge of the stars is interesting in its own right, but because this kind of knowledge frees us from disturbing and erroneous beliefs in astrology, and in the idea that our fate might be written in the stars, an idea that perturbs and unsettles our minds.

KEY FIGURE Epicurus was born in 341 BCE on the island of Samos, an Athenian colony. At the age of eighteen he travelled from Samos to Athens to serve in the army, and then for the next twenty or so years he lived in various parts of the Greek world, both teaching and studying philosophy. He returned to Athens in 307 and set up his famous philosophical school, the 'Garden' (*kepos*). The Garden wasn't just a place where people could go to talk about philosophy: it was a community where Epicurus' followers could live and practise his doctrines. Although Epicurus wrote extensively, very little remains, other than a few letters presenting his doctrines in abridged form, and a few piecemeal fragments. He died in 270 BCE of complications arising from kidney stones. Although in enormous pain, he was said to have remained cheerful until the end, saying that his recollection of his various philosophical contemplations maintained him in a state of happiness despite the obvious suffering.

Two kinds of pleasure

One crucial aspect of understanding Epicurus' philosophical approach to happiness is getting hold of the way he talks about pleasure. To some extent, Epicurus offers a hedonic approach to happiness: after all, his overriding concern is with pleasure or *hedone*. While for Aristotle the thing that we choose for its own sake is flourishing, for Epicurus, we are basically driven by what Bentham calls the two sovereign masters: pleasure and pain.

But it would be a mistake to see Epicurus as a pleasure-seeker or a hedonist in the contemporary sense of the word. The trouble with contemporary hedonism for Epicurus, it could be said, is that it's unintelligent and short-term. If I go out drinking, I may indeed experience pleasure; but the hangover the following morning is a different matter. While you may envy the lifestyle of a film star, the life of a film star in rehab is less enviable.

 What Epicurus was interested in was the idea of taking an **intelligent** approach to pleasure, one that really looked at the pleasures of life, and that tried to make distinctions between them, so that we might be able choose our pleasures more successfully.

So what distinctions can we make when it comes to pleasure? Epicurus says that there are, broadly speaking, two kinds of pleasure. *Kinetic* pleasures are those pleasures that stimulate us, that stir us up, that get us excited: sex, drugs and rock and roll, or whatever the equivalent of rock and roll was in ancient Athens. Kinetic pleasures are the kind of pleasures that send us skittering off in all kinds of odd directions, that unbalance us, that precipitate us into unexpected situations, and that lead to a kind of turbulence of the soul (for Epicurus, the soul was considered to be a physical entity, so this disturbance is not so much meta-phorical as literal). In contrast, *static* (or *katastematic*, to use the technical term) pleasures are not so skittish, changeable or turbulent. For example, we could think of the pleasure of sitting and watching the sun set, the pleasure of enjoying the friendship of another human being, or the pleasures of simple food (cheese in particular!): all these might be relatively static kinds of pleasure for Epicurus.

Kinetic pleasures are those that lead to pain somewhere down the line: they are destabilizing, unsettling and unbalancing pleasures.

Katastematic or **static** pleasures don't cause further disturbance, and help support *ataraxia* (freedom from disturbance).

The important thing to note is that for Epicurus *all pleasure is in itself good*, and *all pain is bad*; but some pleasures are to be avoided because in creating future disturbances, they end up being more trouble than they're worth. For example, Epicurus wasn't opposed to sex, and he admitted that it is one of the pleasures of life; but he noted that nobody's life was, in any significantly lasting way, changed for the better by an orgasm (although you may differ on this point).

The result of this is that if we're to take pleasure seriously, for Epicurus we might need to go easy on the sex, drugs and rock and roll, and to think about cultivating those pleasures that, being relatively more static, don't tend to stir up turbulence in the soul.

 Write a list of as many pleasures as you can think of that you enjoy. Which of these are static? Which are kinetic? Does this distinction say anything useful or interesting about these various pleasures?

Distinguishing desires

In the light of this classification of pleasures into kinetic and static, Epicurus believed it was useful to distinguish between one's various desires to see what kind of pleasures they aimed at.

Here Epicurus adds another level of complexity to his philosophy. When it comes to desires, he says that 'some are natural and necessary, some natural and not necessary and some neither natural nor necessary but occurring as the result of groundless opinion'. What's going on here? Let's start with the idea of necessary desires. 'Necessary', in this context, can be defined as any desire the absence of which might cause actual pain. So, for example, food and water are necessary, but muffins and coffee are unnecessary.

The question of what Epicurus means by 'natural' is a little more difficult to grasp. For Epicurus, 'unnatural' desires are those that don't arise out of our basic physical needs, but that we nevertheless might seek: things such as honour, status and wealth. They are things that, because they aren't rooted in basic need, don't tend towards satisfaction. So if we desire honour, and we get some honour, we want *more* honour; if we want status, and our status increases, then we want *more* status. In neither case are we easily satisfied.

For Epicurus, the primary distinction is between the natural and unnatural desires, between the desire for those things that support our existence and that are capable of satisfaction, and the desire for those things that don't support our existence and aren't capable of satisfaction. The following table gives an idea of how this might work, with some examples of desires from each category:

A: Natural and necessary	B: Natural and unnecessary	C: Neither natural nor necessary
Food (any food) Clothing Shelter	Specific luxury food items Extravagant clothing Mansions and elaborate houses	Honour Status Wealth

Now we can think about these kinds of desire in relation to the two kinds of pleasure. Those desires in category **C** are tangled up with *kinetic* pleasures, because they always project us to further desires. And kinetic pleasures are ultimately more trouble than they're worth. What, then, about the desires in category **B**, those that are natural and unnecessary? Let's imagine that we crave a particular kind of blueberry muffin. If we get the special kind of muffin that we crave, we may be satisfied. But if we pin our hopes upon this kind of muffin, then we may find two things: firstly, in setting our hearts on that one muffin and that one muffin alone, we may cause ourselves significant trouble in tracking it down. And secondly, even after this trouble, we might not be able to actually *attain* the object of our desires, leading to further kinetic disturbance. We might also experience various kinds of disturbing anxiety ('Will they be sold out?' 'What if I can't find any?') because, relatively speaking, the desire for something more specific – for example, a blueberry muffin – is more difficult to fulfil than the desire for something more general – for example, food.

For Epicurus, natural desires are desires for those things that support our existence and that can be satisfied. Necessary desires are desires for those things the absence of which might cause pain. So the desire for food is a necessary and natural desire; but the desire for any one particular *kind* of food is an unnecessary but natural desire.

Desires in category **A**, then, are much easier to fulfil. No muffins? Fine, I'll have a bunch of grapes. Or a slice of cake. Or a piece of bread. Or a pot of cheese. Then I get the pleasure of satisfaction, without the turbulence associated with desires in category **B** or **C**.

An Epicurean experiment

Epicureanism wasn't just a set of ideas about happiness or the good life, but formed a complete approach to the practical business of living. So let's have a look at an Epicurean experiment. This particular experiment takes place over three days.

Day 1
Set aside twenty minutes to do a good job of this part of the experiment.

On a piece of paper spend five minutes jotting down some notes about the various pleasures you have experienced in the last 24 hours. Don't rule out any pleasures for moral reasons, because for the Epicurean, insofar as it's pleasure, all pleasure is good.

Now, on a separate piece of paper draw out two columns. Label one column 'static' and one column 'kinetic'. Take each of the pleasures of the last 24 hours in turn, and put them in the column you think they belong to. Don't be too rigorous about this, but just go with your gut feeling.

Finally, for each pleasure you put in the 'kinetic' section, note down any disturbances that these pleasures led to. When you've done this, go and do something else.

Day 2

On the morning of the next day, return to your list and read over it. In the light of this list, think about the desires that you have for the coming day: in Epicurean terms, are they natural and necessary? Unnatural and unnecessary? Natural and unnecessary? Think about the pleasures that they will lead to: are these static or kinetic?

Now plan out an Epicurean day for yourself. Think about how you can maximize pleasure and attain a greater degree of ataraxia. Consider how you can cultivate static instead of kinetic pleasures. Focus, in particular, on finding pleasure in natural and necessary desires.

Day 3

Repeat the exercise you tried for Day 1. Was your Epicurean day any happier than the day before? Did it lead to more static pleasures? Finally, after 24 hours, take stock and ask if you're any happier.

More to life than cheese?

Of course, with Epicureanism as with everything else, it might take more than a day or two to see if there's enough wisdom in this approach to happiness to make it worth following. Nevertheless, there may already be some questions about Epicureanism that seem perplexing. Our desire for status may certainly be self-perpetuating, but isn't there something natural also in the desire to have some kind of standing in the eyes of others? What does this focus on my own happiness mean for my relationship with other people? And isn't there more to a life well-lived than cheese?

Perhaps; but we don't have to become Epicureans to benefit from the insights of Epicurus.

 The idea that we might respond to our desires with greater intelligence may be of use to us even if we don't sign up to the entire system. There may indeed be more to life than a pot of cheese, a garden, a few friends; but these things, at least, may be a pretty good start.

9. Diogenes the Cynic: the life of a dog

In brief
Another ancient Greek school that has something to say about happiness is that of the Cynics. Taking their name from the Greek word for dog, the Cynics recognized that while human beings are really not very good at happiness, it's something that comes easily to canines. This insight leads to a radical approach to the question of happiness.

What is it about happiness that seems so easy for dogs, and so difficult for human beings?

Look at anybody walking a dog in the park and you'll notice that nine times out of ten the dog seems far, far happier than its owner. While the dog-owner walks along with knitted brows, the dog scampers around chasing pigeons, or leaping into the river, running up to joggers, or – most exciting of all – making friends with other dogs. In fact the dog behaves as if today is the very best day of its entire life. And while not all dogs have happy lives, it nevertheless seems that dogs (and cats too, but let's stick with dogs), given the right conditions, are natural experts in the art of happiness. Dogs seem to have a capacity for enjoying life that we don't. They don't worry about mortgage payments, or the political situation, or whether the economy is in free-fall. They just get on with being dogs. You take them for a walk, and they're delighted. You feed them, and they act as if this is the most brilliant thing that could ever have happened. They're more or less happy to eat anything and to sleep anywhere. They don't spend their spare time reading books about happiness in the hope that this might make them happier.

So what are we missing out on?

This is, essentially, the question that was asked by the ancient philosophers known as the Cynics. Today 'cynicism' has unpleasant connotations, and we might think that a cynic is the last person we could imagine happy. After all, cynicism is popularly associated with a lack of faith in human (or, for that matter, any other kind of) goodness, a belief that people always and everywhere act out of the worst of motives, and perhaps the belief that happiness itself is a waste of time.

But to understand what the Cynic philosophers were up to, we need to put aside the more recent meanings of the term 'cynicism' and go back to its roots. As a philosophy, Cynicism was – at least in the eyes of its proponents, if not its detractors – very different from what we now mean by the word. The name comes from the Greek for dog-like or *kynikos*, and was applied to a group of philosophers who engaged in sometimes shocking pursuits to make their philosophical points. So who were these philosophers, in what way were they dog-like, and what might they have to say about happiness?

 The ancient Cynics (with a capital letter) were not cynics (with a small 'c'): in fact, they were much more optimistic about the possibility of human goodness.

Defacing the currency

Perhaps the most important Cynic philosopher is Diogenes. It's said that Diogenes was sent into exile from his home town of Sinope for the crime of defacing the currency, and thus he travelled to Athens. One story goes that that the reason he committed the crime was that the oracle at Delphi (who seems to have had a reputation for getting philosophers into trouble) said that he should 'give a new stamp to the common currency', and Diogenes interpreted this literally. He seemed unruffled by this change in his fortunes, claiming that if he was sentenced to exile, then the people of Sinope were sentenced to a much worse fate: staying in Sinope.

KEY FIGURE Diogenes of Sinope (404–323 BCE) is one of the more unconventional philosophers of the ancient world. He made it his mission to overturn the assumptions and conventions of the society of his day. He engaged in some radical experiments in living, becoming homeless and taking up temporary residence in a large storage jar in the market-place at Athens. He was apparently kidnapped by pirates and taken to Corinth, where he resumed his simple and sometimes shocking lifestyle. While he was living in Corinth it's said that Alexander the Great came to speak to him. The ruler of the entire known world, and former student of Aristotle, stood in front of the philosopher and asked: 'Is there anything I can do for you?' The philosopher said: 'Yes. Please stand elsewhere, you are blocking out the sunlight.' Alexander apparently sighed, and said: 'Were I not Alexander, I would wish that I were Diogenes.'

After he arrived in Athens, Diogenes attempted to reinterpret the Delphic oracle's words metaphorically, and set about trying to re-mint the coinage of our morals and our values so that we might live better, and happier, lives. Diogenes was a philosopher who attempted to *live* his philosophy. Living in his storage jar in the market-place, he ate, drank, relieved himself and, when he felt like it, even masturbated in full public view, without any concern for what others thought about him. When public-spirited citizens of Athens pointed out that pleasuring oneself in the market-place was not particularly seemly behaviour, Diogenes just sighed and said: 'If only the hunger of the stomach could be sated so easily, simply by rubbing with the hand.'

The way of the dog

But what, you might be wondering, does any of this have to do with philosophy or, for that matter, with happiness? Let's return to the question of dogs. What is it that allows dogs to live happily, but that prevents us from doing so? For the Cynics, the answer was clear: dogs live *naturally*. Unlike dogs, we're trapped by convention, by concern with status, by reliance upon luxury, by our worries about what our neighbours or colleagues might think about us, and by shame. The name 'Cynic', in fact, was first used as a term of abuse; but later it became almost a badge of pride for the Cynic philosophers, who went so far as to bark at those with whom they disagreed.

For the Cynics, happiness comes from living in accord with nature. This means that we need to return to a kind of self-sufficiency and a freedom from convention. The things that we human beings obsess about – wealth, fame, status and so forth – are not necessary to our happiness (here the Cynics are close to the Epicureans). Not only this, but their pursuit leads us away from living in accord with nature. Some food to eat, a little shelter, the relief of bodily urges: the things that we *need* for happiness are relatively few.

Cynicism as a way of living was demanding and far from easy. Cynic virtue was living simply, with a rough cloak to cover you, a small bag to carry a little food, and a stick to help you walk from place to place.

Spend an hour or two hanging out with a dog or a cat. What arts of happiness, if any, can you learn from them? Is there any sense in which 'living like a dog' (or a cat, or whatever other pet you have to hand) might lead to greater happiness?

Citizens of the cosmos

One aspect of this rootlessness (remember Diogenes' barbed comment to the citizens of Sinope) was *cosmopolitanism*, a notion that originates with Diogenes himself: the idea that we might identify not with a particular society or set of conventions, but with the broader world. Diogenes is said to have proclaimed that 'the only true commonwealth is that which is as wide as the universe'. To return to our dogs, a dog is a dog wherever it is, whether in Shanghai or in São Paulo: dogginess pays no heed to local cultural conventions and loyalties. A dog just gets on with being a dog. Dog-owners are natural parochialists; dogs are natural cosmopolitans.

This cosmopolitanism was a place from which the Cynics set themselves up as critics of the society in which they found themselves, because in saying that they were citizens of the cosmos, the Cynics were saying that there was a more fundamental affiliation than that of the city state. This being the case, the Cynic philosophers, for all their disdain of social conventions, didn't seek to withdraw from society, but instead lived the Cynic life right there in the middle of things, pointing out the hypocrisies and the inconsistencies of conventional morality, in their aim to re-mint the currency of ethics and lead people to happiness.

 It's perhaps not surprising that some scholars have suggested that the historical Jesus – an itinerant who lived simply, calling into question conventional morality – was strongly influenced by Cynicism.

Cultivating Cynicism

But is there anything we can do to put the Cynics' philosophy of happiness to the test? I'm not going to suggest that you move into the market-place and satisfy your bodily functions in public, nor am I available to defend you in court if you choose to do so. This is, in fact, a part of the problem with Cynicism: it's a demanding and risky thing to practise seriously. Epictetus, who we will meet in the next chapter, was impressed by the Cynics but also said that there are only a few who have the moral fortitude to truly cultivate Cynicism. It's difficult to live in a storage jar in the market-place; and it's even more difficult to entirely do away with social convention.

And here there lies a kind of contradiction. Dogs, after all, don't need moral fortitude to be dogs. They are just dogs. It seems, in other words, that for us it's natural for that which is natural not to come naturally! In the next chapter we'll explore the later school of Stoicism and ask some deeper questions about this idea of what is 'natural'. But before moving on to look at Stoicism, try exploring the following questions.

THINK ABOUT IT

What might it mean to live naturally? For Diogenes it meant homelessness, relieving oneself in public, and being free of all social conventions. Is this natural? And is this way of living desirable?

---

10. Stoicism: mastering our judgements

In brief

The Stoics were a philosophical school who were deeply influenced by the Cynics; but they asked a question that the Cynics did not explore: if happiness means living in accordance with nature, what does 'nature' itself mean?

Stoicism was one of the longest-lasting philosophical traditions in the ancient Greek and Roman worlds. It was founded by a philosopher called Zeno of Citium.

KEY FIGURE Zeno of Citium (c. 334–c. 262 BCE) was said to have been stranded in Athens after a shipwreck. There he wandered into a bookshop and read about the philosopher Socrates. He didn't buy the book; instead he asked the shop owner where he could find a real, live philosopher. The owner directed him to the philosopher Crates, a Cynic. Zeno combined the Cynic concern with living naturally and the emphasis on reason he found in the philosophy of Socrates, Aristotle and Plato. He eventually started giving lectures at the *Stoa Poikile* or 'painted porch' in Athens, and it was this that led to these philosophers becoming known as Stoics: those who met by the painted porch.

Zeno took up the problem of what the Cynics actually meant when they talked about what was 'natural'. As we've seen, dogs don't seem to have to choose to live in this or that fashion. They get on with being dogs. But when it comes to us, we seem to be strangely distanced from what's natural, if only because we, unlike dogs, can ask the question: *What is the natural way of being human?*

The problem for Zeno was that, if we can't answer this, then all attempts at a kind of natural way of living seem to be on shaky foundations. As a result, Stoicism has three main concerns. The first is *logic*. If we're to understand nature, we need to be able to reason clearly, and the Stoics were important in the development of philosophical logic in the ancient world. The second is what might be broadly called *physics*, a study of the way the universe works, so that we can put our logic to good use in establishing a firm understanding of what we mean by 'nature'. And the third is *ethics*, because this isn't just a matter of understanding what's natural, but also of adjusting our behaviour in such a way that we live in accord with the way that things actually are.

REMEMBER THIS!!!

The ancient Stoics were concerned with three major questions: **logic** (the question of how we reason); **physics** (the question of how the world works); and **ethics** (the question of how we are to live).

A guide to life

The Stoics were a highly successful philosophical school, and flourished in both Greece and Rome. Here we'll look at the philosopher and some-time slave Epictetus, whose book the *Enchiridion* is one of the classics of Stoicism, and one of the clearest guides to Stoic experiments in living.

The *Enchiridion* is a guide to life that aims to make us better able to cope with the difficulties we might experience. For Epictetus, one of the main problems we face is that we're inclined to spend too much time getting upset about aspects of the world over which we have absolutely no power. The *Enchiridion* begins with the words: 'Some things are up to us and some are not up to us.' Some of the things not up to us might include whether we're slaves or not, whether we're born in this or that place, whether we're sick or well, even our reputations and our possessions. Those things that are up to us, according to Epictetus, include our opinions, our ideas, our impulses and our desires.

KEY FIGURE Epictetus (CE 55–135) was a Greek slave who lived in Rome. His owner gave him permission to study philosophy, and later Epictetus gained his freedom and began to teach philosophy. He was a famously good speaker, and became a friend of the Emperor Hadrian; but according to the accounts, although he had friends in high places, he nevertheless lived extremely simply. His famous *Enchiridion* was compiled by his pupil Arrian.

The distinction between those things that are up to us and those things that are not is important when we face practical problems in daily life. So, for example, Epictetus asks his readers to imagine that they want to go to the bath house. Roman bath houses were boisterous places, full of 'people who splash, people who jostle, people who are insulting, people who steal'. This boisterousness, as can be imagined, was often annoying and upsetting. But Epictetus reminds us that we can't change the culture of the bath house. It's not up to us. What we can change are our opinions, expectations and judgements. 'What upsets people', Epictetus says, 'is not things themselves, but their judgements about things.' We get upset because we think that people *shouldn't* jostle, that they *shouldn't* splash, that they *shouldn't* steal, even if we know very well that, people being people, they will.

So what's the answer? For Epictetus, it's to accord our reason with the way that the universe works.

Epictetus says that it's hopeless to try to bend the entire world to fit with our desires. Instead, peace of mind and happiness come from training our desires so that they are in accord with the way the world is.

One way of according ourselves with what is actually the case is by resisting the tendency to make **value judgements**. Value judgements are ways of adding to the situation in which we find ourselves. So, for example, Epictetus says that when we see that we're wealthier than somebody else, we tend to assume that we're superior. But no, he says, we should simply say that our wealth is greater and leave it at that. Anything else is just adding unnecessary judgements to the situation. When we see somebody drinking lots of wine, it's better to simply say that this person drinks a lot of wine, instead of saying that they're a drunk and that they really shouldn't drink so much. If somebody insults us, the problem lies not in the words themselves, but in 'the judgement about them that they *are* insulting'. If we realise that we're going to die, we shouldn't judge it as terrible, but simply say, 'I'm going to die', and not load this fact with moral judgement.

A Stoic experiment

But can this contribute to our happiness? Stoicism has always been a popular philosophy in times of trouble; it doesn't fit well with the feel-good 'you can transform your life' style of some contemporary approaches to happiness, because Stoicism recognizes that sometimes you *can't* transform your life. Often we don't just want happiness – we want success, glory, fame, better health. And some books even promise that you can have it all. Stoicism is interesting because it doesn't offer any of these things. Instead it says (echoing the Cynics' lack of concern with worldly success) that even without these things, there's no reason not to be happy. It's true that the Roman Emperor Marcus Aurelius was a Stoic – Stoicism, unlike Epicureanism, doesn't mean turning away from success – but then so was the slave Epictetus, which suggests that Stoic happiness is more or less independent of worldly fortune and misfortune.

 Think of some activity in which you take part regularly – the contemporary equivalent of going to the bath house – and think of the times that you have found aspects of this activity unpleasant: the things that have made you irritable, or that have disturbed your mind. Now write down the following:

- How much of what annoyed you was inherent in the nature of the situation? (For example, you may have been in the cinema, and people were chatting behind you. Or you may have been in a meeting, and people were using annoying jargon. But these things may simply be what happens in cinemas and at meetings.)
- How much of what was happening was up to you (in Stoic terms) and how much was not up to you?

Now, before you attempt to embark upon the activity again, read over your notes and recollect those things that are inherent in the situation, and those things that you can change. Then continue with the activity as before, but with the following difference:

- For those things that are inherent to the situation and not up to you, remind yourself that this is what happens – they are a part of the necessity of the situation.
- For those things that concern your response to the situation, ask yourself what you can change to diminish the frustration.

Finally, when you return home, reflect on your experience. It might help to write your reflections down, as the Stoic philosophers used to. How successful were you in recognizing the necessity of the situation and in training your mind not to become disturbed?

If you do this over a period of time, and if the Stoics are right, you should succeed in fortifying your mind to the extent that even the most jargon-filled meeting or the chattiest of cinema audiences fails to disturb you.

---

11. Thomas Aquinas: that old time religion

In brief
*The approaches to happiness we've looked at so far are all focused on decidedly this-worldly questions about how we go about the business of leading our lives. But is there more to happiness than human action and happiness **here and now**? In this chapter we look beyond these worldly concerns to ask about happiness in relation to the idea of God and to religious belief.*

The dimension of transcendence

One domain of happiness we haven't yet considered is that of religion. We're perhaps all familiar with the story of the convert who moves from a life of abject misery to a life of happiness after finding God, or after putting on the robes of a monk, or after learning how to practise Sufi dancing. And while until now much of the discussion of happiness has focused on ordinary, everyday, worldly practices, it's worth asking whether these are, in the end, insufficient. Do we need, in other words, something otherworldly, something *transcendental*, if we're to be happy?

In his book *Authentic Happiness*, the co-founder of positive psychology Martin Seligman proposes that some notion of transcendence, spirituality or religion is necessary to the good and happy life. By 'transcendence' he's not referring exclusively to religion, but instead says that it's a matter of reaching out 'to connect … to something larger and more permanent: to other people, to the future, to evolution, to the divine, or to the universe'. This could, in other words, be God; but it could equally well be a Cynical (in a philosophical sense) kind of cosmopolitanism, a Stoic kind of reason, or an Epicurean kind of understanding of the nature of things. This claim that some kind of transcendence is necessary for any theory of happiness does, however, raise the question of whether religion might at least *help* us be a little bit happier.

Transcendence is a term that's sometimes used in studies of happiness to talk about a dimension *beyond* that of our own personal life and concerns. This could be a religious dimension, but it could involve commitments to other things such as politics, the arts, the sciences, or to a wider sense of society or community.

The current research on the relationship between religion and happiness doesn't yet seem to have reached any clear consensus. Part of the problem, of course, is that 'religion' is a broad category (and 'transcendence' is, arguably, even broader), covering so much of human life that it may not even be *meaningful* to say that religion is necessary for, or contributes to, happiness. If we're saying that religion contributes to happiness, we need to ask what aspects of religion we're talking about. So instead of asking, 'Does religion contribute to happiness?', we should ask a more careful question: 'What, if anything, is it about this particular religion that contributes to happiness?' And, for balance, the opposite question: 'What, if anything, about this particular religion gets in the way of happiness?'

There's another philosophical problem here that's worth mentioning, and that's the question of the relationship between the truth-claims of religion and the supposed happiness of adherents. So, let's say for the sake of argument that a particular religion *does* seem to make its adherents happy. This doesn't make that religion *true*. Indeed, the religion could just be what Plato called a 'noble lie' that keeps people happy at the expense of the truth. In such a case, is that particular religion desirable or not?

Have a look at the following exercise.

Think about the idea of transcendence, the connection we have to 'something larger and more permanent: to other people, to the future, to evolution, to the divine, or to the universe'.

- Write down any aspects of transcendence there may be in your life. In what sense are they aspects of transcendence?
- Now choose one and reflect on how these aspects of transcendence relate (if they do) to your happiness. Are they necessary for your happiness? If so, how? If not, why not?

A fat monk and a flying ass

The definition of 'transcendence' talked about in positive psychology is rather broad. Here we're going to narrow things down a little to look at one particular idea of transcendence: the idea of God. There's good reason to narrow the question down in this way. Although the religious practices in which human beings are involved are startlingly diverse, many philosophers in the West, when they ask whether religion and happiness might be related, are not asking about religion *in general* but instead about one question above all others: the question of God. The model of religion taken by philosophers, as a glance at any philosophy of religion textbook will demonstrate, is often surprisingly narrow: for philosophers in the West the philosophy of religion is often a matter of exploring the philosophical question of how we might think about an omnipresent, omnipotent, and probably *male* creator God. So, for present purposes, this is the question that we will be asking: does believing in such a God, and does involving oneself in the kind of pursuits that those who believe in such a God involve themselves in, lead to happiness?

To answer this question, let's go back a little way to the Italy of the Middle Ages, the age of the monk Thomas Aquinas.

KEY FIGURE Thomas Aquinas (1225–74 CE) holds the crown of being the greatest philosopher of the medieval European world. Born near Aquino in Italy, he became a monk in the Dominican order and studied with the philosopher Albertus Magnus (1206–80 CE). Thomas was a man of prodigious learning who attempted the impressive task of synthesizing the knowledge from the pagan ancient Greeks, in particular the works of Aristotle, with the Christian teachings of the Bible. It was said that Thomas could dictate four different texts on four different topics to four different scribes, all at the same time, turning from one to the other in turn. This story seems implausible until you look at a bookshelf containing the enormous body of his life's work. And then you begin to suspect that this might, in fact, be true.

There's a particularly charming story about Thomas Aquinas told by the writer Umberto Eco. Thomas was prodigious not only in his learning but also in his girth, and one day when the brotherhood were sitting eating dinner, the other monks decided to play a trick on the overweight monk. So they ran to the window and shouted, 'Thomas! Thomas! Come quickly! There is an ass flying past the window!' Thomas, wanting to see this miracle for himself, stood up and wobbled over to the window and looked out. There was no ass. The other monks thought this was tremendous fun, but Thomas reprimanded them. 'I would rather believe in a flying ass', he said gravely, 'than I would in a lying monk.'

Flying asses apart, Aquinas is a philosopher who interestingly explores the connection between the question of happiness and the idea of God. But to see how he sets about this, we need to return to the work of Aristotle.

The fragility of happiness

While the Stoics have an austere vision of happiness in which it's possible to be happy in the face of almost *any* misfortune, for some philosophers this is unreasonable: remember Aristotle's claim that Priam may have been virtuous but was simply unlucky. Happiness in the world, for Aristotle, is something that's never assured; it's a somewhat fragile thing. This being the case, the best we can do is to make sure that we practise the virtues that give us the best possible chance for happiness. Beyond this, however, happiness is not within our control.

For Aquinas, when he comes to reading Aristotle, this is something of a problem. The problem is this: if happiness is the final end of human life, then it's a final end that's nevertheless subject to chance. This is not to say that Aristotle believes that happiness is completely unstable. The whole point of Aristotle's theory of happiness is that there's an awful lot that we can do; but at the same time, there's something in this notion of happiness that seems to pull in the opposite direction to Aristotle's claim that happiness is 'complete in itself'. Not only this, but for Aquinas, for happiness to be a *final* end there must be a kind of happiness that isn't subject to this kind of uncertainty. 'Happiness', Aquinas writes, 'is that perfect good which entirely satisfies one's desire; otherwise it would not be the ultimate end, if something yet remained to be desired.'

For Aristotle, happiness was always dependent, to a degree, on luck. For Aquinas, this suggested that worldly happiness was not dependable and could not, therefore, be a final end. So Aquinas claimed that there was a happiness *beyond* the happiness possible in the world.

If Aquinas has a problem with the fact that the happiness Aristotle promises is a less complete thing than Aristotle himself might like, there's also at least implicitly a problem in the early Christian tradition's notions of happiness, in that happiness in this world is seen as almost entirely unimportant – a house built upon sand, in the image taken from the Sermon on the Mount – in comparison with the happiness of the world to come. Indeed, if you read the Sermon on the Mount it's hard not to suspect that what's being recommended is that we should turn away from *all* concerns with worldly happiness for the sake of a greater happiness to come.

> 6:19 Lay not up for yourselves treasures upon earth, where moth and rust corrupt, and where thieves break through and steal:
>
> 6:20 But lay up for yourselves treasures in heaven, where neither moth nor rust corrupts, and where thieves do not break through nor steal:
>
> 6:21 For where your treasure is, there will your heart be also ...
>
> ... 6:25 Therefore I say unto you, Take no thought for your life, what you shall eat, or what you shall drink; nor yet for your body, what you shall put on. Is not the life more than food, and the body than clothing?

Within the context of very early Christianity, when the Kingdom was expected to arrive *any minute now*, this approach to happiness made sense, and there are still some Christians who claim (although not entirely convincingly) that worldly happiness matters not at all. But against these views, Aquinas recognized that there *was* in fact happiness in the world, and that this happiness needed to be accounted for.

This led Aquinas to a neat solution.

 There *is* happiness in the world, Aquinas acknowledged, but this happiness is limited. There's the happiness that comes from eating a good meal, enjoying a beautiful sunset, or sharing somebody's friendship. But these things don't represent an ultimate fulfilment of our desires. To have such fulfilment, to have the possibility of an ultimate, unchangeable happiness, there needs to be a good thing that is itself ultimate and unchangeable. In other words, *there has to be God*.

What this allows Aquinas to do is, on the one hand, to claim that the ultimate happiness lies in God, a happiness to which no other happiness comes close, and on the other hand to recognize that there are very many good things in the world, very many causes for happiness, and that worldly happiness also matters. It also allows Aquinas to claim that he has surmounted the problem in Aristotle – the problem of Priam who is virtuous but unfortunate – precisely because the misfortune of the likes of Priam is a worldly misfortune that will pass away (as in the Sermon on the Mount) to be replaced by a greater, indeed an *ultimate*, happiness to come.

Happiness meanwhile

Worldly happiness, then, is for Aquinas always incomplete and imperfect; but this doesn't make it worthless. Nevertheless, both the happiness itself and the objects of this happiness are transient. So the happiness that comes from friendship, a good meal and so on will pass away as surely as will the meal and the friendship themselves. But here Aquinas distinguishes between two different possibilities for worldly happiness.

 The first possibility arises out of living virtuously, a happiness open to all of us. This is how Aquinas allows a place for Aristotle and non-Christian philosophers within his philosophical system. This happiness is, as Aristotle always recognized, to some extent contingent. However, for Aquinas there's a much more robust kind of worldly happiness, and this is open only to the faithful. This second kind of worldly happiness comes about only through divine grace. For Aquinas, a life lived in hope and expectation of the life to come is *already* blessed.

One might ask how these two visions of happiness – the vision of a happiness of virtue, and the vision of a happiness of virtue infused by divine grace – differ in character. For Aquinas, one difference is the relationship that it's possible to have with suffering in each case. If this idea of a happiness infused by faith conjures up images of glassy-eyed smiles and tambourines, this is far from Aquinas' intent. Let's return to Priam.

In the first sense of worldly happiness, that Aquinas might attribute to Aristotle, Priam is virtuous but unfortunate, and so although he has put the conditions in place for happiness, he hasn't been lucky and happiness has eluded him. And this is the end of the story. Sometimes, things just don't work out. But now imagine (putting questions of anachronism to one side) Priam infused by the divine grace of which Aquinas speaks. How does the grace-filled Priam differ from the grace-less Priam? Here we go back to those puzzles in the Sermon on the Mount, the 'beatitudes' in which poverty, meekness and mourning are seen as forms of *blessedness*. In other words, for Aquinas, the suffering of the grace-filled Priam is a suffering that is not only redeemable but already redeemed, even while he suffers. Indeed, there's even a sense in which, if ordinary worldly happiness is a route that seeks to avoid suffering, the higher happiness Aquinas writes about is happiness *by the way of suffering*, as in the Christian story the Cross is said to lead to the sublime happiness of Resurrection.

 One interesting idea from Aquinas is that happiness may involve a *greater awareness of suffering*. In what sense might this be true? Is there a danger that the idea of 'ultimate' or 'perfect' happiness might lead to us undervaluing more ordinary, everyday happiness? What might be the problems with this?

Aquinas for the faithless

According to Aquinas, then, the happiness of the faithful trumps the happiness of the faithless any time. The arguments he provides are, however, persuasive only if one accepts the overall context of his thinking. As Saint Anselm said: 'I believe so that I may understand.' It's not that theological arguments necessarily aim to persuade others to believe (something they usually do badly), but instead that on the basis of belief they seek understanding. This implies that such arguments may *never* be persuasive to non-believers. So, for example, I might say: 'Fine, Aquinas claims that the faithful are happier: I can accept that.' I might even be persuaded that there's evidence to support this. Nevertheless, I might conclude that this seems like a somewhat crass reason to convert.

There is, however, a value in asking about Aquinas' insights into happiness beyond the obviously religious context of his thought. Aquinas brings home the full force of Aristotle's recognition of the contingency of happiness even in the most virtuous of lives. This highlights the limitations of notions of happiness that tie together virtue and happiness. But Aquinas also raises some fascinating questions about the relationship between happiness and suffering. Our everyday idea of happiness may involve the avoidance of suffering; but perhaps if we're interested in more robust and lasting happiness, we need to reflect more deeply on the possibility of suffering. In the next chapter we will move from medieval Italy to ancient India, to explore this question further.

12. Buddhism: getting away from suffering

In brief
In the following three chapters we will move from the philosophical traditions of Europe to those of India and beyond, in particular to the traditions of Buddhism. Buddhism has always concerned itself with both happiness and suffering. But what does this ancient tradition have to say to us today?

A method for happiness?

In the contemporary literature of happiness, one tradition seems to stand out more than all the others, and that's Buddhism. It has become almost a truism that the teachings and practices associated with Buddhism might be capable of revolutionizing our approach to happiness; and it's often stated that the contemporary science of happiness is not so much *discovering* how happiness happens but instead *rediscovering* what was already well known in the traditions of Buddhism. No self-respecting book on happiness, it seems, is complete without a reference to the Buddha.

So what *can* Buddhism tell us about happiness? What kind of idea of happiness is there in the Buddhist tradition? And, more importantly perhaps, what, if anything, can the methods of Buddhism do to help us cultivate happiness?

Who was the Buddha?

To understand Buddhism, we need to go back to the figure of the Buddha. Most books about Buddhism tell how the Buddha was born Siddhārtha Gautama, the son of King Śuddhodana and Queen Māyādevī, in the Śākyan kingdom just to the south of the Himalayas. After his birth, a holy man predicted that the boy would either become a great saint or a great king; and because Śuddhodana wanted an heir for himself, he became determined that Siddhārtha should not leave home in search of sainthood. As a result he provided the boy with every pleasure imaginable. Certain Buddhist texts take delight in describing the intense sensual pleasures to which Siddhārtha was exposed. Yet one day, the prince left the palace and travelled through the streets of the city, and there he saw a sick man, an old man and a corpse. He was plunged into anguish, an anguish that led to his departure from his life of luxury and a relentless quest for truth. Eventually, sitting underneath a tree in a place now known as Bodh Gaya, in present-day Bihar, India, he experienced an awakening (the Indian term *bodhi* is somewhat better translated as 'awakening' than 'enlightenment'), which liberated him once and for all from the sufferings of the world. The remainder of his life was spent teaching the 'four noble truths': the truth of suffering, the truth of suffering's causes, the truth that there is an end to suffering, and the truth of the path that leads away from suffering.

So much for the legend. More sober historical research suggests that much of this is probably later invention. So what do we know about the *historical* Buddha?

KEY FIGURE The Buddha is the title given to Siddhārtha Gautama, who lived some time around the fifth century BCE, although the exact dates are in dispute. He was from a small republic to the south of the Himalayas. At this time in India, there was a strong tradition of wandering philosophers who would leave their homes and embark on an extraordinary range of experiments in living. Siddhārtha joined their number, according to one of the earliest accounts, while he was 'still young, a black-haired young man endowed with the blessings of youth in the first stage of life'. After an experience that he referred to as his awakening, he founded a community of followers who practised and passed on his teachings. He died, according to some accounts, in his eighties, of food poisoning.

In addition to this somewhat skeletal biography, we also know a great deal about the Buddha's teachings, or at least about the teachings that were codified by his followers in the years following his death. And it's these teachings that have drawn the attention of modern-day happiness researchers.

The problem of suffering, or, happiness by the back door

Although Buddhism does sometimes talk in positive terms about happiness, more often it can be found talking about the path *away* from that which impedes our happiness, in other words the path that leads away from suffering. Suffering, indeed, is the central problem in Buddhism; and if we're to understand what Buddhism has to say about happiness, then we need to know a bit more about what's meant by suffering in the traditions of Buddhism.

The term for 'suffering' in the Pāli language of the earliest Buddhist texts is *dukkha*. However, the Pāli term has slightly broader meaning than the English 'suffering'. So extreme physical pain may entail *dukkha*, but so may nagging anxiety brought on by a deadline, or the frustration of forgetting where you've left your keys.

Dukkha or 'suffering' in Buddhism doesn't just mean pain. Instead it has a much wider reference, encompassing various forms of pain, suffering, dissatisfaction, disquiet, disappointment and discontent.

Dukkha in Buddhism isn't really a matter of unpleasant *feelings*. In Buddhist psychology it's recognized that there are both pleasant and unpleasant feelings, as well as those that are neither strongly pleasant nor unpleasant. It's also recognized that the coming and going of these feelings is often largely outside our present control, and is the result of previous conditions, not all of which are (or ever were, perhaps) within our power. If we're bitten by a snake, for example, there will be intensely unpleasant feelings associated with the bite. If we eat a delicious meal, we may have intensely pleasant feelings associated with the meal. The pleasure and pain arise out of the conditions that have gone before.

So where does *dukkha* or suffering come in? Suffering comes in when we get involved in either holding on to pleasant feelings or pushing away unpleasant feelings. Have a look at the following case study.

Jessica was always interested in Buddhism, and so was excited when she got the chance to travel to Thailand and to live alone in a forest retreat, far from the nearest hospital. Unfortunately, while she was meditating one day, she was bitten on the leg by a centipede. The pain was excruciating. Jessica lay on her bed, sweating with fever and waiting for the pain to pass. 'Why me?' she thought. 'It's so unfair! Why did I come to Thailand? It was a stupid thing to do! I'm an idiot.' Then a dark intention formed in her mind. 'Death to all centipedes!' she muttered feverishly.

But then she realized: on the one hand there was the physical sensation, that strange, intense burning feeling in her calf; but beyond the physical sensations, there was a whole bundle of suffering caused by self-recrimination, by centipede-cursing, by fear, and by attempting to push away the raw fact of pain. Jessica took a deep breath and she started, very carefully, to take her attention to the burning pain in her leg. Her mind become more settled. The hours passed ...

What's going on in this story? One way of looking at it is this: if you're bitten by a centipede, you can do nothing about the physical sensations themselves. They're simply a part of the fact of having a body. But in the Buddhist view the suffering (which isn't the same as the raw painfulness) lies not in the physical sensations so much as in the mental disquiet that you experience in relation to these sensations. In early Buddhism, in particular, the Buddha often suggests paying attention to the experience of bodily sensations while undercutting the mental commentary. As one text puts it, we should train ourselves so that 'in the seen will be merely what is seen; in the heard will be merely what is heard; in the sensed will be merely what is sensed; in the cognized will be merely what is cognized' – a form of training that might also be approved of by the Stoics over in Greece and Rome.

But it's not only unpleasant sensation that risks causing suffering. So does pleasant sensation. In this case we don't push away sensation but try to keep hold of it. But once again, it's our desire to hold on that causes us misery. Think of the pleasure we get out of being on holiday, and the way that this pleasure can be undermined by the dark cloud of our knowledge of our impending return and the fact that we want to hold on to this blissful state of freedom from responsibility.

Four truths

This brings us to the so-called 'four noble truths' that are so central to Buddhist doctrine. What are these truths? And in what sense, if any, are they 'truths'? Sometimes the four noble truths are expressed like this:

- Life is bound up with, or entails, suffering or disquiet;
- The root cause of this suffering is craving;
- There is an end of suffering which is awakening;
- Buddhism provides us with the path to awakening.

But in the same way that arguments about God are convincing only to the converted, this view of suffering is perhaps unpersuasive to any but the most hard-bitten of Buddhists.

One arguably more useful way of thinking about these four 'truths' is in the fashion recommended by scholars in the tradition of Tibetan Buddhism, who, instead of seeing these four things as abiding philosophical truths about the world *in general*, claim that they can be used as a way of classifying phenomena. The distinction may seem subtle, but it's a useful one. If we look at the four truths like this, then, when we come across something within our experience, it's a matter of asking ourselves the following questions:

- Is this a 'suffering'?
- Is this a cause of suffering?
- Is this the cessation of suffering?
- Is this a way towards the cessation of suffering?

 To explore this approach to experience, try the following exercise. At the end of the day, think about your experiences over the past few hours. Can you classify them as *dukkha*, causes of *dukkha*, cessations of *dukkha*, and ways towards the cessation of *dukkha*? Use the following table if it helps. It might be that columns 1 and 3 deal more closely with experience and columns 2 and 4 deal more closely with actions or activities.

1. *Dukkha*	2. Causes	3. Cessations	4. Ways towards cessation

Now ask yourself the following questions:

- Does this classification make sense of your experience and activities in any meaningful way?
- Does it help you find ways to deal with the problem of *dukkha* (suffering, discontent or disquiet)?
- What are the implications of this approach for how we think about happiness?

But what about *happiness*?

It can often seem that Buddhism is *much* more directly concerned with suffering than with happiness; but we should remember that *dukkha* has an opposite: *sukha*.

KEY TERM

The word *sukha* is often encountered in the Buddhist texts as a part of the compound *hita-sukha*, meaning well-being and happiness. The early Buddhist texts, at least, recognize that there's a kind of well-being that we can attain here in the world, which is why the often-repeated claim that 'Buddhism says that life is suffering' is mistaken. However, one of the insights of the Buddhist tradition is that if we fail to take account of suffering, then we're not going to attain to well-being.

We often imagine that suffering and well-being are opposite poles, and that we have to turn away from the former to attain the latter. What the traditions of Buddhism ask of us is that instead of attempting to simply suppress suffering, or trying to forget it, we should look as closely as we can at the suffering that we experience, and inquire about its origins and how we might best respond to it. The really urgent issue is not *finding happiness*, but *removing the immediate causes of suffering*. And if we do this, then we might find that it's to our benefit and our happiness.

TRY IT NOW!

This is an exercise in paying attention to the push-and-pull that, according to Buddhism, tends to characterize our experience.

Firstly, set aside a morning or a whole day and, during the course of this day, pay particular attention to painful and pleasant sensations. Notice how you naturally want to *keep hold of* pleasant sensations, and how you naturally want to *push away* painful sensations. See if you can distinguish between the sensation itself, and the push-and-pull response.

Once you've become good at making this distinction (if there is such a distinction), see if you can keep your attention on *just the sensations* rather than the responses.

And when you've done this, consider the questions below.

- Does it make sense to distinguish between raw sensation and the various responses we might have to these sensations?
- On the basis of your experience, do you think there's any truth to the claim that this push-and-pull is the cause of suffering?
- Imagine if you could just experience the sensations without this kind of response (like Jessica just experiencing the raw sensations of pain). Do you think this is possible? And would this, as the Buddhists claim, be a kind of freedom from suffering?

So far, we've looked in general terms at the approach to happiness and suffering in the traditions of Buddhism;

but one thing that makes Buddhism particularly interesting to researchers today is that it provides a *method* for responding to the *dukkha* that seems inherent in life; and that method is meditation. This, then, will be the subject of the next chapter.

13. Traditions of meditation

In brief
One of the methods for responding to the question of suffering in Buddhism is meditation. Currently there's a revived interest in meditation as a means to happiness, and many books recommend that meditation can help us attain a higher degree of happiness. So what is meditation? And is there anything in these claims?

The happiest man alive?

Matthieu Ricard's left prefrontal cortex is, it has been said, remarkably frisky. Ricard is a French monk and trained biochemist who was ordained within the tradition of Tibetan Buddhism. In the year 2000 a group of scientists from the Center for Affective Neuroscience in Madison, Wisconsin prevailed upon him to have a number of sensors attached to his conveniently shaved scalp, so that his brain activity could be measured. It turned out that Ricard's left prefrontal cortex exhibited unusual levels of activity. As philosopher Owen Flanagan wrote in an article for *New Scientist* in 2003:

> The left prefrontal lobes of experienced Buddhist
> practitioners light up consistently (rather than just
> during meditation). This is significant, because

persistent activity in the left prefrontal lobes indicates positive emotions and good mood, whereas persistent activity in the right prefrontal lobes indicates negative emotion. The first Buddhist practitioner studied by Davidson ... [Ricard] showed more left prefrontal lobe activity than anyone he had ever studied before.

It's thanks to this research that Ricard has developed a reputation in the global press for being the 'happiest man alive'; although as both Ricard and Flanagan have pointed out, there are problems with the claim that happiness can be somehow objectively measured by activity in the prefrontal cortex. Nevertheless, evidence not only from long-term meditators such as Ricard but also from research with less experienced meditators suggests that meditation may contribute to increased mental and physical well-being.

But the claims about the benefits of meditation raise a number of questions. The first is: *What kind of meditation?* The English term 'meditation' is a slippery one, and even if we restrict ourselves to the Buddhist tradition, we find a wide range of practices that could be called 'meditation', and a number of different terms in the languages of traditional Buddhism that might be translated into English as 'meditation'. So what kind of meditation helps, or do all of them?

The second question is: *How much meditation?*

THINK ABOUT IT It may be that Matthieu Ricard is the happiest man alive, but as a monk he has also done rather more meditation than most of us have time for. He is, in other words, a virtuoso meditator. But becoming a virtuoso isn't something that all of us are capable of. Perhaps monks who meditate a lot are happier; but not all of us would be happy to be a monk who meditates a lot. This raises the question of whether meditation is a worthwhile investment of time for those who aren't monks. In the Buddhist traditions in the past, meditation was often seen as a specialist pursuit.

The third question, too often overlooked in meditation research, is: *Are there any down-sides?* In other words, does meditation have any undesirable side-effects?

Before we answer these questions, it might be useful to define a little more precisely what we mean by 'meditation'.

(At least) two kinds of meditation

Perhaps the broadest definition we can give of meditation is that it's a practice that aims at the self-regulation of the body and mind. The presence here of *both* the body and the mind is important. Meditation isn't just a matter of mulling things over – it also involves a physical discipline: meditation is a matter, in other words, not just of the mind, but of our entire organism.

Although this idea is almost forgotten in philosophy today, in ancient Greece this would have been widely recognized. As the philosopher Aristippus wrote, 'bodily training contributes to the acquisition of virtue', as it does to the ability to perceive and direct one's thoughts. Various Greek philosophers philosophized in different postures: Socrates, for example, was often found standing in an almost complete trance for hours on end. Similarly in India and China, there are long traditions of connecting disciplines of the mind with disciplines of bodily training.

Meditation can refer to a wide range of practices, but the best general definition we can give is that meditation is *a form of bodily and mental discipline that aims at self-regulation.*

The self-regulation that happens in meditation usually works by directing the attention in various ways. Here it's useful to make a distinction between two different approaches to meditation: **concentration** meditation and **investigative** meditation. Concentration meditation aims to bring about a more concentrated state of both body and mind, and a degree of stillness and focus; investigative meditation, on the other hand, is concerned with a more analytical approach to experience. Within Buddhism this distinction roughly corresponds to the distinction between *samatha* ('calming' or 'tranquillity') meditation and *vipassanā* ('investigative' or 'insight') meditation. The chart below gives a rough outline of the two approaches.

Samatha	Vipassanā
Calming	Insight
Stilling of experience	Analysis of experience
Concentration	Investigation or questioning

A couple of more concrete examples might make this clearer. A common form of concentration meditation is what is known as *ānāpānasati*, often translated as the 'mindfulness of breathing'. What this involves, at its most basic level, is sitting down and training the mind to become sensitive to the coming and going of the breath. Over time it's possible to develop the ability to keep the attention focused unwaveringly on the breath, leading to a stilling of the body and the mind. Sometimes this is talked about as a 'calming' meditation, although 'calm' is perhaps misleading. The state that is aimed at is a kind of relaxed alertness, rather than the state of calm you might have on a Sunday morning in bed.

Conversely, one common form of investigative meditation involves sitting quietly and attending to whatever appears in your own experience, noting the rise and fall of experiences without attempting to affect them in any way or to theorize about them. This kind of meditation is analytical or investigative in that it requires a sharpness of attention that can distinguish often very subtle elements of experience, and also in the sense that it has a kind of questioning edge in the way that it seeks to refine this sharpness of attention.

It may be useful to think of these not as wholly different *kinds* of meditation, but instead as different *aspects* of meditation. Some meditation practices may have a stronger investigative element, while some may have a stronger element of bringing about a physical and mental calming. And the two, more or less, support each other: a degree of calm and stillness is needed for us to be able to investigate experience with more precision.

The following exercise has elements of both calm and investigation.

Although meditation is a discipline that can take years to learn, the following exercise, adapted from the early Pāli Buddhist texts, may help you explore the distinction between these two aspects of meditation.

Set aside ten minutes for this exercise. First find a secluded place (free from human, animal, electronic or other distractions) and sit – either on a chair or on cushions – with your spine relaxed but upright.

- Take a few moments to settle into your posture, becoming aware in particular of the various sensations in your body.
- Now, once you're settled, let your eyes close, and bring your attention to the sensations of the breath. Let the breath come and go naturally – don't try to force it in any way – but simply pay attention to the quality of the breath, and the sensations in your body as you breathe.
- When your attention is settled on the breath, introduce an element of investigation. Notice whether the breath is warm or cool, heavy or light, long or short. Pay attention to how your thoughts and feelings change with the breath's rise and fall. Notice how the body moves with the rhythm of the breath. In other words, take an active interest in the processes of breathing that you normally might take for granted.
- Whenever your attention wanders, bring it back to the breath, allowing the sensation of breathing to settle your body and mind.
- After ten minutes, relax your attention, and take another minute or two to reflect on your experience.

Do you feel different to how you felt before you tried the meditation? If so, how? Do you feel calmer? Happier? More contented? Less happy? What difficulties did you have in the meditation? What things got in the way of being able to pay attention to the breath?

The effects of meditation are said to be cumulative over time (and the research supports this), so you shouldn't expect immediate results. You may find that the meditation has helped a little, or not at all. However, if you're to explore meditation more deeply, it's worth asking what, in the light both of current research and of the traditional accounts, the effects of meditation might be, and how it may help to support happiness. We'll look at this next.

Although the exercise in this book is a start, the best way of learning meditation is by studying with an experienced teacher.

The benefits of meditation

The early Buddhist texts list an impressive number of reasons why you should think about meditating. Meditation, they say, helps you sleep well; it helps boost concentration; it makes you unperturbed in the face of death; it makes you more attractive to others; it does away with bad dreams; it helps you endure pain; and, if you get really good at it, it allows you to walk through walls and mountains 'as if through space', to dive in and out of earth as if it were water, to walk on water as if it were land, to fly through the sky cross-legged; and it gives you the power (should you need it) of being able to stroke the sun and moon with your bare hands.

Sadly, not all of these claims stand up to scrutiny. Nevertheless, some of the more sober claims are plausible and increasingly supported by the evidence. Meditation is now routinely used within healthcare settings as a means of dealing with pain-management and pre- and post-operative anxiety. Studies have also suggested that meditation may be of benefit for everything from depression to cardiovascular disorders to dermatological conditions. There's some evidence that meditation is of benefit in diminishing stress, in improving reaction times, in ability to respond to adversity, in empathy, and in the reported levels of subjective well-being of those who practise it. Not only this, but studies such as the one in which Ricard participated suggest that meditation leads to significant physiological changes.

Some questions about meditation

But let's come back to our initial questions about meditation. We have, to some extent, addressed the first question: 'What kind of meditation?' But despite the growing body of research, we don't yet know with enough precision what kinds of meditation, in conjunction with which other factors, correlate with precisely which kinds of benefits. And in the meditation supermarket, it can be difficult to choose: do you go for a Tibetan, Sri Lankan, Korean or Japanese flavour? What are the benefits of each?

REMEMBER THIS!!! To say that meditation, broadly, is beneficial is not greatly more useful than saying that medicine, broadly, is beneficial: we would be wise to ask which medicine is useful under precisely which conditions.

The second question, 'How much meditation?', also needs further investigation. Some of the largest claims made for meditation arise out of research on those who have practised meditation for many thousands of hours. It's not clear how useful or practical meditation may be, and what the benefits might be, for those of us who have decided not to commit ourselves to this intensive practice. Is a little meditation, in other words, worthwhile? While it does seem that we don't need to all be virtuoso meditators to experience some benefits from meditation, we should remember that for much of the history of Buddhism it was often considered a much more specialist pursuit.

The third question is perhaps even more important: 'What are the down-sides?' Many researchers are much more interested in establishing the benefits of meditation than asking about the possible detriments, despite there being some evidence that meditation may not be wholly beneficial. There are, for example, accounts of undesirable side-effects in a minority of cases, ranging from *increased* anxiety, confusion and negativity, to experiences of guilt, suicidal and destructive behaviour, and – my favourite

– *grandiosity*. Even in the ancient Buddhist texts, there are some fascinating accounts of certain kinds of meditation having fairly severe side-effects. The Buddha once recommended a particularly strong form of meditation, on the stages of the decomposition of the corpse, to a group of monks who became so distressed by the practice that they committed suicide.

THINK ABOUT IT Think about some of the views of the good life that we've already explored in this book. Which of them fit well with the practice of meditation? Which of them, if any, don't fit so well? We've defined meditation as a 'bodily and mental discipline that aims at self-regulation'. Are there other activities that might fit this description (one example might be physical training and sport)? If so, what, if anything, makes meditation *different*?

Of course, the answer to the question about the potential benefits and down-sides of meditation will depend on what one's own conception of the good life is. There may be conceptions of happiness and flourishing that don't fit particularly well with the practice of meditation, or at least not with the practices drawn from the Buddhist tradition. Meditation practices may not just lead us to the good life, but also shape our idea of what the good life is.

IF YOU REMEMBER ONE THING While there are good reasons for the claim that certain forms of meditation can be of benefit when it comes to health and well-being, there's no reason to think that meditation is a panacea.

14. Śāntideva: happiness and compassion

In brief
It can sometimes seem, when reading about Buddhism, that
happiness and suffering are simply one's own affair, as if the
ultimate purpose of Buddhism is one's own liberation from
misery and suffering. Here we turn to some later Buddhist
traditions to explore the intriguing idea that there may be a
connection between happiness and altruism; and we return
again to the paradox of hedonism.

Sometimes, when thinking about happiness, we can see it
as our own individual possession, something that we *own*.
Maybe you're happy, and maybe you've done a great deal
of meditation so that your left prefrontal cortex is pecu-
liarly frisky: but why should that be any concern of mine?
Sometimes the objection is levelled against Buddhism
that it is, ultimately, self-serving, in that it's concerned with
individual liberation from suffering. Of course, it's not just
Buddhism that's open to this charge. In fact, a great many
approaches to happiness could be seen as a kind of self-
interest. This raises the question: what about the happiness
of other people? What, in other words, about **altruism**?

To answer this question, let's turn to one of the greatest poets and philosophers of the Buddhist tradition, the

8th-century monk Śāntideva. It was Śāntideva's insight that happiness and suffering *cannot* simply be my own affair. Part of the reason for this is that the happiness and suffering of others have an effect on our own happiness and suffering. For Śāntideva, it's not possible to be wholly happy while others around us are suffering. If this is the case, then it's not only *not nice* to consider only one's own happiness, but it's also incoherent. 'When happiness is liked by me and others equally', he writes, 'what is so special about me that I strive after happiness only for myself?'

According to Śāntideva, if happiness is a problem *for us*, then we need to recognize that it's a problem *for all of us*.

And for Śāntideva, one important aspect of happiness is that it's not a zero-sum game. My increase in happiness doesn't mean your decrease in happiness, nor does your increase in happiness mean my decrease in happiness. So it makes sense to strive for happiness *in general*.

KEY FIGURE Śāntideva is the author of the book known as the *Bodhicaryāvatāra* or the *Guide to the Bodhisattva's Way of Life*, one of the most important and widely read of later Buddhist texts. We know very little about the author himself, although it seems that he lived around the 8th century and studied at the Buddhist university of Nālandā. Although the version of the *Bodhicaryāvatāra* that we have today has clearly been edited by other hands, at the heart of it is a striking, original and individual voice.

In the absence of anything like a proper biography of Śāntideva, we're left with the colourful legends. It's said that Śāntideva was a former prince who became a monk. In the monastery he was renowned (rather like Thomas Aquinas) as much for the size of his belly as for his dedication to meditation and study. In fact, according to the Tibetans, he was known to his contemporaries as 'Bhusuku', a nickname that translates as 'eats, sleeps, shits', because this seemed to be an apt summary of his contributions to the life of the monastery. One day, in an attempt to shame the fat monk into demonstrating his ignorance, he was invited to lecture to the entire assembly. Śāntideva took his seat and began to recite the verses that now make up the *Guide to the Bodhisattva's Way of Life*. The monks were astonished. They had expected stammering and nonsense, but Śāntideva's verses were profound and deep. So profound were they, in fact, that in the middle of reciting them, during a philosophically tricky section of the text, Śāntideva began to levitate, and then disappeared, his voice continuing to resound from the sky until the text came to a close.

Śāntideva and the paradox of hedonism

So much for the legend. What concerns us here is why Śāntideva claims that the desire for happiness can't be limited to our own individual happiness.

One reason may lie in the paradox of hedonism that we've already encountered – the idea that attempts to aim directly at happiness often miss the mark. If this is indeed true then, as the Buddhists have long recognized, there's a risk that in setting itself up as a path that leads away from suffering, Buddhism might serve only to *increase* our suffering; in focusing on my own happiness, Buddhism might actually lead away from happiness. This is a particular issue in Buddhism because of the claim that suffering arises out of the push and pull that we experience in relation to pleasant and unpleasant experience. Śāntideva puts this in the strongest terms: 'All those who suffer in the world do so because of their desire for their own happiness.' But then he goes on to make a further intriguing statement: 'All those happy in the world are so because of their desire for the happiness of others.'

For Śāntideva, techniques that aim at our own happiness lead inevitably to suffering. So if we care about our own happiness, we should care about the happiness of others. Do you think this is true? Can you think of any examples of times when aiming for your own happiness led to its opposite? Can you think about times when working for the happiness of others led to your own happiness?

What is interesting is that with the second statement about wishing the happiness of others, Śāntideva effectively doubles the paradox of hedonism. Not only do we *not* get happiness from looking for happiness, but the *only* way to happiness is to think about the happiness of others.

A second reason why focusing on individual happiness might be self-defeating is what might be called the *viral* nature of happiness. There's increasing evidence that states of mind have a strongly social dimension. Both unhappiness and happiness rub off on others. If we spend time in the company of people who are happy, we find ourselves cheering up; if we find ourselves falling in among the cheerless, again this tends to colour our perspective. This is, of course, wholly unsurprising: indeed, it would be surprising if it was *not* the case, as we've evolved to be social beings, to respond to the cues provided by others.

Taking these two things together, this suggests that if we care about our own happiness, we need to think about the happiness of others. Here we might come up against a philosophical objection. Surely, we might say, wishing for the happiness of others *for the sake of our own happiness*, using the happiness of others as a means to an end, is still subject to the paradox of hedonism? The best way to respond to this is to call into question the philosophical tendency to see an absolute distinction between altruism and self-interest. If happiness is indeed something that's not an individual possession but fundamentally *shared*, then the ideas of absolute self-interest and absolute altruism make no sense. So even if there's an element of self-interest to our wish to deliver others from suffering and act for the happiness of others, this self-interest doesn't diminish the altruism of our action. *Indeed, the right kind of self-interest might actually be altruistic, and the right kind of altruism might be in our own interests.*

It's Friday evening, and I get a phone call from a friend.

'Hi', he says. 'Can you do me a favour?'

'Sure', I say. 'What is it?'

'I'm painting the back of my house. Can you come and give me a hand this Saturday?'

I hesitate. I was looking forward to a quiet weekend reading. I picture ladders (I don't like heights), hours on end with pots of paint, and I realize I'd rather stay at home. I've had a rough couple of weeks. I *need* the break. But I simply *can't* let him do it on his own.

So I agree, and the following morning I catch the train.

And everything I feared is just as I thought it would be: the heights, the long hours of hard work, the heady smell of paint – everything except for one thing. While half-way up a ladder, paintbrush in hand, I realize that I'm happy, happier than I was the week before, or the week before that, far happier than I would have been had I stayed at home. Liberated from the narrow confines of my own concerns, for a moment I'm happy precisely because I've stopped worrying about my own happiness.

Śāntideva's claim that the desire for the welfare of others leads to happiness and the desire for our own welfare leads to suffering is one that we can put to the test.

Firstly, write down three things you can do for the benefit of your own (not somebody else's) happiness. Now, over the next three days, carry out one of these tasks each day. Make notes on whether this has provided you with the happiness you had hoped for, and if so, how.

Next write down three things you can do for the benefit of somebody else's happiness. Over the next three days, carry out one of these tasks a day. Again, note whether, and to what extent, these things have led to happiness.

Finally, ask yourself which of these activities were more worthwhile? Which led to greater happiness for yourself? For others? Does this make you inclined to agree with Śāntideva, or not?

15. Confucius: ritual

In brief
If it is indeed the case that happiness is not a personal possession but something that has to exist in a wider context, we have to ask what kind of context is the best for human happiness. To explore this question we'll move from India to China, to meet the philosopher and sage Confucius, who proposed a vision of how it might be possible to achieve harmony, and thus happiness, within human society.

Confucius is perhaps the most important philosopher in Chinese thought. He famously summed up his life in the following words: 'At fifteen, I had my mind bent on learning. At thirty, I stood firm. At forty, I had no doubts. At fifty, I knew the decrees of Heaven. At sixty, my ear was an obedient organ for the reception of truth. At seventy, I could follow what my heart desired, without transgressing what was right.'

KEY FIGURE Confucius was born in what was then the state of Lu, in present-day Shandong province, some time around 551 BCE. The name 'Confucius' is a Latinized version of his Chinese name: Kong Fuzi. The philosopher's early life was marked by tragedy:

his father died when he was still young, and he was brought up, if not in poverty then at least in impoverished circumstances, by his mother. He was a member of the social class of low-ranking scholar-officials, and while in Lu he took on a number of relatively lowly official positions, including posts that involved responsibility for public granaries and pastures.

After the state of Lu fell under foreign control, Confucius left his home town and took to the life of a travelling teacher. He was concerned in particular with the nature of virtue and the question of what might constitute a moral government. Confucius travelled around China, which was at the time politically fractured, in an attempt to find a local ruler to whom he might act as an advisor. He continued to travel and to teach until his death in the year 470 BCE.

Confucius' own life was overshadowed by repeated difficulty and disappointment, and when he died, it was with a sense of failure in his mission to restore the virtuous era of previous government. Nevertheless, his thought became one of the most enduring formative influences of Chinese culture down to the present day.

So what does this disappointed wandering teacher and low-ranking official have to say about happiness?

Confucian happiness

One reason why it's worth exploring Confucius in a book on happiness is that Confucius was a resolutely political thinker. He was concerned not so much with the question of how I might *personally* live well and happily, but with politics at all levels. By this I mean that he was concerned not only with the question of how the state should be governed, but with the question of how we relate collectively to each other in all contexts: as members of the same family, as teachers and students, as government officials, rulers, citizens and subjects.

Confucius' vision of the past is important for understanding his approach to the question of happiness. In today's China, many look back to Confucius as a paragon of virtue and a symbol of a more morally upright time in the past. However, Confucius himself, back in the 5th century BCE, was also looking back to the era of the Zhou dynasty and earlier, which he believed offered more moral and more virtuous examples of government and public life. In the good old days of the early sage-kings Yao and Shun, Confucius claimed, there simply *was* no need to worry about teaching morality, because this was an era of spontaneous harmony in which, without doing anything at all (Confucius talked about *wu wei*, literally 'non-action', an idea that would later be associated with Zhuangzi, who we will meet in the following chapter), justice and order prevailed.

Wu wei is a term meaning 'no action' or 'non-action'. It appears in both Confucian philosophy and in Daoism (see next chapter). It doesn't suggest sitting around doing nothing. Instead, it's a way of acting that is fluid, harmonious and without any kind of struggle.

In the same way that the natural world moves in an orderly fashion without the need of any external forces, back in the day, Confucius maintained, so did the human world. But to regain this harmony is a long task: it was not until the age of 70 that Confucius says his own desires accorded with 'what is right'; but it's precisely this ability to desire that which is right and harmonious that constitutes happiness for Confucius. Happiness, in other words, is a profoundly **moral** issue.

Ritual

Happiness, for Confucius, is rooted in the core virtue of *ren* – 'humaneness' or 'benevolence' (sometimes in older books this is written *jen*, both being transliterations of the same Chinese character). *Ren* is not simply a *feeling* of benevolence, it's also something manifested in the way that we *act* towards others.

How, then, are we to maintain *ren* or humaneness, and thus ensure happiness for ourselves or others? The answer given by Confucius, or at least a part of the answer, is *li* or ritual. Remember that for Confucius, the fundamental problem is the disorder of our lives and our relationships, in contrast to the orderliness of the natural world and, supposedly, of the previous age of the sage-kings. In the absence of such a natural, spontaneous order, ritual is a way of bringing a new kind of orderliness to our lives.

Ren is the Confucian term meaning 'humaneness' or 'benevolence'.

To some, perhaps, the idea of ritual may seem restrictive and limiting. But the best way of getting a sense of what Confucius means is by thinking about the rituals in which we involve ourselves, and that we value.

Think of three different kinds of rituals that take place regularly in society (for example, the rituals of the court-room, or the rituals of a sports match, or the rituals of shops or restaurants). In what sense do you think these rituals contribute to harmony and happiness? What are the negative aspects of these rituals?

Ritual doesn't have to be oppressive. Instead, it can be a way of making the best of us. Think how we disapprove of the lack of sportsmanship when players disrupt the ritualized moves that take place in sport. The ritual framework of a game of football or tennis is in part a way of guaranteeing that, in the heat of the moment when passions are running high, the participants don't slide into disorder. Another example might be the rituals of the classroom that ensure good relations between teachers and students.

Before reading on, note down three different kinds of shared (rather than personal) rituals that are important to you in your life. Now think about them. Why do they matter? How do they help bring order and happiness to your life?

Living musically

One way of seeing ritual is as a kind of social performance akin to music. If you go and see an orchestra perform, you might be profoundly impressed by the harmony, the beauty and *the sense of freedom* that comes from the swelling music. But this is possible precisely *because* of the orderly, ritual nature of orchestras. What you probably wouldn't do is see the members of the orchestra as oppressed, even though their every move is dictated by the score.

Ritual, at best, can be seen as similar to the musical score followed by an orchestra. It's something that allows us to perform together harmoniously. But, of course, not all rituals are good rituals, in the same way that not all scores are good scores. Confucius was a powerful critic of many of the rulers of his time, who took the reins of power without manifesting any of the responsibilities. In a very famous passage, he argues that what's needed is a 'rectification of names', a determination to make one's conduct conform to the roles that one has assumed: so if I'm called a ruler, I should pay attention not to my own enrichment, but to ruling well; if I'm called a parent, I should fully assume the responsibilities of being a parent.

Music and happiness

What has this to do with happiness? Here the analogy of the orchestra is again useful, and it brings us really rather close to Confucian thinking. Music was one of Confucius' central concerns, and he believed that it was essential to moral development. Like a parent listening to the sound of their teenager's music blaring from upstairs, Confucius worried that *the wrong sort of music* led to the formation of the wrong sort of character. Music, because it has a direct effect on our moods and states of mind, is an important way of regulating our passions and according us with a proper state of harmony.

The Chinese character for music (樂) is also the same as the character for 'happiness' (although the pronunciations are different). Perhaps this indicates a deeper connection between happiness and music, both of which (in the Confucian vision) involve harmony.

The harmony that comes from music, for Confucius, is allied with a kind of joy, happiness and ease. There's a tale that Confucius was once so overwhelmed by a sense of harmony after listening to some music that for the following three months he didn't notice the taste of meat, never having before imagined that music could be so beautiful. The joy occasioned by the music was itself enough to return him to the kind of harmonious existence characterized by the natural world, and that existed in the time of the ancient sage-kings.

Confucianism is often presented as a grim and rigorous doctrine; but the idea of happiness as a kind of music, a harmony that involves not just myself but others, is not without a kind of beauty. But this is also a utopian notion: Confucius never managed to bring about this vision of a harmonious society. And here we should ask some questions of this Confucian idea of happiness, the foremost of which is this: *What about discord?* After all, there is perhaps also a value in discordance, in absence of harmony; and if we take the analogy of the orchestra seriously, then we have to ask: *Whose tune is it that we're playing?*

 Rituals can both free us and imprison us. The tune that sounds sweet to one set of ears may sound discordant to another. And it may depend, in part, upon where one is seated in the orchestra.

16. Zhuangzi: a philosopher of uselessness

In brief
Now we will turn to another Chinese philosopher, Zhuangzi, whose approach to happiness was very different from that of Confucius. For Zhuangzi (as for the Epicureans) there was something inherently unconducive to happiness about involvement in the broader social and political worlds; as a remedy, Zhuangzi offered the proposition that we should be gloriously, splendidly useless.

One of the criticisms sometimes made of contemporary psychological and philosophical approaches to happiness is that they're part of a much broader culture of aspiration that is, at root, self-centred and acquisitive. Once you've sorted out the career, the house, the car, the beautiful spouse and perfect children, the regular holidays in the sun and the pension fund to keep you in old age, you can turn your attention to thinking about happiness. In this kind of view, the good life seems like something we can just add on to our beautiful, successful lives. The message is this: not only can you be the fabulously wealthy CEO of a multinational corporation, but you can be happy and wise at the same time. Happiness becomes another consumer product, another means to, and indication of, success.

THINK ABOUT IT Today happiness is often related to success, but do happiness and success always go together? Are there times when being *less* successful might make us *more* happy?

There are some good reasons why we might seek to resist this vision. While it would be mean-spirited to begrudge happiness to wealthy CEOs (or, for that matter, to anyone else), there's a danger that if we see happiness, success and virtue as necessarily entailing each other, we risk assuming that those who are successful must be either happy or virtuous or both. But this sits uncomfortably with many approaches to happiness in the ancient world, both East and West. It's true that Marcus Aurelius was both a Stoic philosopher and the emperor of Rome. But his happiness (to the extent that he was happy) was very much a Stoic kind of happiness. If you prefer the kind of happiness that comes from hanging out with the Epicureans eating cheese, your chances of becoming Emperor are seriously diminished.

This raises the question of whether there might be certain kinds of happiness that *conflict* with the desire to keep the house, the car, the high-powered job, the beautiful spouse and so on. Of all the philosophers, nobody manages to puncture our aspirational approaches to happiness with quite as much verve and with such a winning combination of mischief, wit and sharp-wittedness as the Chinese Daoist philosopher of uselessness, Zhuangzi (sometimes

158

written Chuang-tzu). For those of us who fret continually about spending our time usefully, reading Zhuangzi is an unsettling experience. For if he attempts to persuade us of anything, it's that happiness doesn't come from being useful. Instead, happiness comes from precisely the opposite of usefulness, from making ourselves thoroughly useless.

THINK ABOUT IT Which approaches to happiness that we have explored so far seem to fit *best* with the idea that success and happiness might go together? Which fit least well? Think of the times that you're being useful and the times that you're being useless. When, in general, are you happier?

The mysterious philosopher

Zhuangzi is the name given to the purported author of the work that's also called the *Zhuangzi*. The *Zhuangzi* is one of the core texts of the Daoist tradition of philosophy, a name that comes from the Chinese term for 'way' or 'road', *dao*.

KEY FIGURE Scholars are still arguing over the historical Zhuangzi, but most are agreed that the seven so-called 'inner chapters' of the book known as *Zhuangzi* can be attributed to a single author who lived around the 4th century BCE, while the remaining chapters are considered to be the work of writers from later generations. This makes the author of the 'inner chapters' of the *Zhuangzi* a rough contemporary of the philosophers who were arguing about the good life in Athens.

The *Zhuangzi* is written, unusually for a work of philosophy, largely in fables and stories. These are sometimes strange, occasionally puzzling and paradoxical, frequently overtly philosophical and – all too rare in philosophy – often funny. Zhuangzi appears as a central character in many of these fables, and as a literary creation he's a strange figure, both deeply serious and scatological, profoundly concerned with the moral problems of his time and also with a good appreciation of slapstick and the absurdity of everyday life. The subtlety of his arguments and the strangeness of his stories are largely the reason for his enduring fascination.

Dragging one's tail in the mud

Let's look at one of the stories about Zhuangzi, to get a flavour of the kind of philosophy with which he's associated.

One day, as Zhuangzi was idling by the river fishing, a couple of officials turned up, sent by the king of the ancient kingdom of Chu. 'Are you Zhuangzi?' they asked. Zhuangzi nodded. 'We would like you to become a minister in Chu', said the officials.

Many would have leapt at the chance for political power, but Zhuangzi hardly budged an inch. 'There is in the temple in the state of Chu a sacred tortoise', he said. 'This tortoise has been dead for three thousand years, its shell wrapped in silk and placed in a carved box. It is honoured in the rituals of the temple, where even the king makes offerings to it. But tell me this ...' Here he paused. 'Would the tortoise rather be honoured in this way, or to still live, dragging its tail in the mud?'

The officials had to concede that the living tortoise had the better deal. 'In that case', said Zhuangzi, 'clear off, and leave me alone to drag my tail in the mud.'

On the uselessness of certain trees

Chinese courts were often dangerous places to spend one's time, characterized by intrigue, power struggles and uncertainty. So there's some wisdom in Zhuangzi's decision to drag his tail in the mud: high-status roles, even if we aspire to them, come at a cost.

 Research on baboons has found that high-status individuals – the alpha males of the baboon world – have consistently higher levels of stress hormones than baboons of middling status. If you're a baboon, the best bet is to be neither at the top of the pile nor at the bottom, but somewhere in the middle.

Zhuangzi's proposal is rather more far-reaching than this. He suggests, somewhat in the fashion of the Cynics, that we should evade the status game altogether. But unlike the Cynics, he recommends that we shouldn't even attempt to hold up a moral mirror to society. We should simply give up on making ourselves useful and wander freely, doing as we choose. This isn't so much a matter of becoming *low*-status as of becoming *no*-status.

This emphasis on uselessness has more to it philosophically than it first seems. In chapter four of his book, Zhuangzi tells several stories about large and apparently useless trees. In one, a carpenter called Shi notes that a vast tree at a shrine is nothing more than 'worthless lumber', too twisted, too full of holes and gnarls, too oozing with sap to be put to any use. Later the tree appears to the carpenter in a dream and says to him: 'Look at all those other trees that are useful: they are cut and pruned and die young; but I've been trying to be useless for a long time. And although it almost killed me, I've succeeded. Can you imagine how useful it has been to me to have attained uselessness?'

 Can uselessness really be useful? Can you think of any examples? Think of those people you know who are most concerned with status and success, and those who are least concerned with these things. Which group of people, in general, is happier?

Nourishing one's life

The problem with trying to be useful, for Zhuangzi, is that in bustling around and doing useful things, we literally wear ourselves out. Whether what we're doing is aiming at happiness through cultivating ourselves inwardly, or aiming at happiness through a concern with our outward status and success, either way, we risk failing to nourish ourselves and courting exhaustion. Struggling for happiness, by whatever means, we miss out on it. Our life becomes impoverished and undernourished; we find ourselves lacking in vitality: our life becomes less *lively*.

It's not that the 'way' or the *dao* of Zhuangzi leads us anywhere in particular, or even that it's something that we have to do. Instead, quite the opposite is true. What causes all the trouble is our attempt to get somewhere, our attempt to do something, our attempt to use our life usefully, to attain to particular goals.

 To live a truly nourished life, for Zhuangzi, we need to forget about struggling to be happy, about the various techniques and methods for cultivating happiness. We need to forget also about trying to get anywhere at all. When we do so, it's life itself that directs us, life itself that decides for us.

The idea that life should have goals or end points is deeply rooted in Western thought. We can see it's already there in Aristotle with his way of questioning what the end or purpose of things might be. It also crops up again in much of the writing in the realm of positive psychology, where it's repeatedly said that happiness comes, in part, from the fulfilment of goals. But what if the setting of goals is itself a large part of the problem? This is the question that Zhuangzi wants us to ask ourselves.

THINK ABOUT IT Is it true that setting (and achieving) goals is a necessary part of happiness? Is there any sense in which the setting of goals could *diminish* our happiness? What are the implications of the idea that existence may have *no goal*? Some people see this possibility as a reason for gloom, but it seems that for Zhuangzi this thought is potentially one that can free us up.

Rum in the afternoon

Zhuangzi goes further than simply acknowledging the paradox of hedonism. He recognizes that if we want to be happy then we have to stop aiming at happiness. But he also calls into question the very idea of existence having a goal, whether this is happiness, power, success, flourishing or anything else. What if there *is* no goal for existence? Or, to put things rather differently, what if, as the scholar of Chinese thought François Jullien writes, 'the pursuit of any goal, the quest for any end, even happiness, wastes vitality'? If so, then when we put our goals to one side, rather than this becoming a way of us nourishing our own lives, *our own lives end up nourishing themselves, of their own accord.*

CASE STUDY

When I think of Zhuangzi, I think of a man I met almost a decade ago when I was working as a door-to-door researcher for a university, asking old people in a poor neighbourhood of a large British city about their subjective well-being.

I knocked on the door and an elderly Jamaican man answered. 'Hello', I said, 'I'm doing a survey on happiness.'

'Happiness?' he chuckled sceptically as he invited me in.

We sat in the kitchen and I started to go through the questions. 'Do you feel as if you have achieved your life's goals?' I asked. He giggled. 'What a ridiculous question!' he said. I tried again. 'Would you say you are a) always happy with how your life is going, b) usually happy with …' He interrupted me. 'Who thinks of these things?' he said. 'Have some rum!'

He poured us both a large glass of rum. It was two in the afternoon. Fortified by the rum, we continued with the questionnaire. Every question seemed to provoke in him enormous fits of giggles. We clinked glasses, we drank, I filled in the answers in an increasingly unsteady hand. And by four o'clock, when I wobbled back out into the sunlight and he waved goodbye, I had to conclude that perhaps, *just perhaps*, I'd spent the afternoon with the happiest man in existence.

I suspect that the man I was talking to hadn't read Zhuangzi; but then I suspect that he didn't need to. Somehow, in his sheer liveliness, in his lack of concern with my strait-laced questioning, he managed to say something about happiness that brought me back down to earth, something that had nothing to do with questionnaires, with the notion of subjective well-being, or with the idea that life is a game in which we must struggle for success.

It seems difficult to put to the test whether Zhuangzi is right or not. After all, if you start setting goals to see if cultivating this kind of useless activity contributes to happiness, you're already doing precisely the opposite of what Zhuangzi recommends. Cultivating uselessness is difficult: remember that the tree tried to be useless for a long time, and the effort almost killed it.

The following exercise may help to explore some of the questions raised by Zhuangzi.

Firstly, take an hour during the day when you have nothing scheduled, and decide to call it an hour of uselessness. If you find yourself wanting to plan something during this period, remind yourself that this is time dedicated to being useless and is not to be filled with useful activities.

166

Now the difficult part. When you get to the period of uselessness that you've decided on, simply see what happens. Don't do anything for any particular purpose. Instead of thinking, 'What should I do next?', ask yourself: 'Hmmm, I wonder what I'll do next?' And go with whatever comes up. Every time you find yourself wanting to be useful or setting a conscious goal, just let yourself say: 'Ah, forget it. I'll just see what happens.' Perhaps you'll go ice-skating, although you've never skated before. Perhaps you'll go and sit with a coffee somewhere and watch the world go by. Perhaps you'll just stand there, without a thought in your head. Perhaps you'll board a flight to China in pursuit of Zhuangzi. Who knows?

Finally, a little later, give yourself time to reflect on your period of uselessness. What was it like? Were you happy or unhappy? What happened when you tried to put conscious goals to one side? Did you manage it?

If you get good at this kind of exercise, you might be able to stretch your practice of uselessness to a whole afternoon. Or even a day, a week, a month, a year. You might even spend the rest of your days happily dragging your useless tail in the mud.

17. Mencius: a different kind of happiness

In brief
Our final philosopher in this book is another Chinese thinker and a follower of Confucius' teachings: Mencius. Mencius asks some interesting questions about the external conditions that we may need for happiness. Taking up Confucius' concern with government, he explores the question of the relationship between happiness and politics.

The name 'Mencius', like 'Confucius', is a Latinized version of a Chinese name. Mencius is known in China as Meng Zi, and his philosophy takes up some of the questions we've already seen in Confucius. But in other ways it makes genuinely new departures – and it's on the question of what kinds of conditions might be needed for human flourishing that Mencius makes the greatest contribution.

KEY FIGURE Mencius lived in the early Warring States period, around the 4th century BCE. Other than legends (legends that mirror, to some extent, the stories of the life of Confucius), we know little about the first few decades of Mencius' life, although it's said that he was a disciple of Confucius' grandson, Zi Si.

Whatever his early life was like, Mencius later went on to teach, seeing himself – as had Confucius before him – not so much as an innovator as a transmitter of teachings from the past; but this time the teachings were those of Confucius himself. More fortunate in his political career than Confucius, Mencius became for a period a High Minister in the state of Qi, but the king of Qi refused to take his advice and, unhappy with being an advisor whose advice was ignored, he resigned. He spent the remainder of his days teaching small groups of disciples.

Although Mencius, like Aristotle, was interested in human flourishing, the notion of flourishing that he used was rather different. For Mencius, human nature was naturally inclined towards goodness, given the right conditions; but the problem that Mencius was preoccupied by – and one that may be of contemporary relevance – was that this natural inclination depended upon external conditions to come to fruition. If the external conditions aren't there, then goodness, flourishing and happiness are difficult, if not impossible.

Sprouts, virtues and hungry oxen

In arguing that we're naturally inclined towards goodness, Mencius uses a metaphor drawn from the observation of nature: that of plant growth. We all have, he writes, four 'sprouts' of virtue.

KEY TERM

According to Mencius, virtue has four 'sprouts' (*duan* in Chinese). The word *duan* means the 'growing tip' of a shoot, but it also has the figurative meaning of 'beginning'. The four sprouts of virtue for Mencius are: a sense of compassion; a sense of shame; a sense of respect; and a sense of right and wrong.

As an example of how these sprouts might be innate, Mencius asks us to suppose that we see a child about to fall into a well: in seeing such a thing, we would be moved to act for the child's welfare. The reason for our acting would not be wanting favour from the child's parents, nor a desire for fame, nor a dislike of the sound of drowning children, but because we have a natural tendency towards compassion for others.

These four sprouts, in Mencius' account, can be developed into flourishing virtues. But here we come up against a problem. How is it that there are people who don't act for the welfare for others? How is it that *we ourselves* often fall short of this flourishing, virtuous life? To answer this question, Mencius proposes another thought-experiment. It's worth quoting in full, as it's such a lovely passage:

> The trees of Ox Mountain were once beautiful. But because it bordered on a large state, hatchets and axes besieged it. Could it remain verdant? Due to the respite it got during

the day or night, and the moisture of rain and dew, there were sprouts and shoots growing there. But oxen and sheep came and grazed on them. Hence, it was as if it were barren. Seeing it barren, people believed that there had never been any timber there. But could this be the nature of the mountain?

When we consider what is present in people, could they truly lack the hearts of benevolence and righteousness? The way that they discard their genuine hearts is like the hatchets and axes in relation to the trees. With them besieging it day by day, can it remain beautiful?

If the right conditions prevailed, Ox Mountain would be richly forested, as the hills of much of the world were richly forested before the grazing of large herds of sheep and oxen. And even now, *sprouts* grow up on Ox Mountain; but then the cows and sheep come and nibble away at them, and so the mountain remains bare and treeless. If, on the other hand, we fenced off the mountain, and let it return to its natural state, we would find that within a generation or so it would be reforested. So it is with our natural propensity to flourish: we may be made for flourishing, and flourishing, however we conceive of it, may be the natural end of human life; but if the external conditions are wrong, these sprouts of virtue can find themselves stunted and incapable of growth.

THINK ABOUT IT What is Mencius trying to say about human nature in his story about Ox Mountain? Do you agree? Think about the image of the cattle that come and graze. Mencius seems to be suggesting that our capacity for flourishing is *continually* being nibbled away at. If this is the case, then what might the things be that prevent us flourishing? Are they internal or are they external?

Tugging our sprouts

Although Mencius doesn't specifically address the question of *happiness* in his work, he does talk explicitly about the good life. 'Benevolence', he writes, 'is people's peaceful abode. Righteousness is people's proper path.' And his work raises some interesting points about the search for happiness that we've been exploring here. The first is the issue of the hedonic paradox: how a desire for flourishing or happiness might be the very thing that gets in the way of happiness. And the second is the broader *political* conditions that may be necessary for happiness and for a fullness of human life. We'll look at these in turn.

Mencius' version of the hedonic paradox (although we must remember that Mencius' notion of flourishing is less a matter of hedonic pleasure than of living virtuously) is, once again, expressed in a story, this time about a farmer from Song. In ancient China, the people of Song were often the butt of jokes and satire, on the grounds of their supposed lack of intelligence.

> Once there was a man from Song who planted some seeds. The seeds sprouted, but the man became impatient. So he went into the field one day and tugged at all the sprouts to make them grow more quickly. The following day, he returned to his field to find that the sprouts had all withered and died.

If flourishing is 'natural' (and this claim raises all kinds of complex philosophical questions), then any attempt to force flourishing is doomed to failure. Here we can perhaps see a correlate of Zhuangzi's notion of naturalness, and of action through inaction. The sprouts grow *by themselves*. We may need to provide them with helping conditions (keep away the bugs, make sure they're watered and so on), but the growing isn't something that we have to force. 'What I dislike about wise people', Mencius writes, 'is that they force things.' Here Mencius is close both to Confucius, who was concerned with the *naturalness* of government in the time of the early sage-kings, and Zhuangzi, who was aware that life must *nourish itself*, and that this cannot be forced.

This has implications for some of the approaches to happiness we've been exploring. Many of these approaches, from the point of view of Mencius' thinking, may be attempts to *force* the development of a flourishing life, and thus be ultimately counter-productive.

Can you think of any examples (in your own life or in the lives of people you know) of this 'tugging at the sprouts'? What was the result? Was it useful or counter-productive?

Mencius' philosophy is at root *optimistic* about the possibilities of human nature. Given the right conditions, we will all be good, flourishing and happy. Do you agree with him?

But there's something else interesting in Mencius' approach to human flourishing, and it's this: if human beings are inherently given to flourishing, *given the right conditions*, then the quest for a flourishing and happy life is fundamentally political in nature. And that leads us to our second question.

The politics of happiness

Mencius forces us to ask what kind of state or government might be the best in terms of human flourishing and happiness. But what if we don't accept Mencius' claim that the sprouts of virtue are inherent in everyone? Perhaps some people are, in the genetic lottery, born bad or born sad, or both. There may be certain kinds of minds that are just less well inclined towards virtue or happiness. As always, this is probably not a question of nature or nurture, but instead a complex set of interactions where genetics and culture meet.

REMEMBER THIS!!! Even if we don't take Mencius' claim about the sprouts of virtue at face value, he nevertheless reminds us that the happy or flourishing life isn't just a personal quest upon which we must embark, but also a question of the kind of **world**, the kind of **culture**, that best supports this flourishing.

Both as a philosopher and as a political adviser, Mencius was always profoundly concerned with the kind of state that would lead most to the flourishing of those in it. And his observations are still pertinent today:

> In years of plenty, most young men are gentle; in years
> of poverty, most young men are violent. It is not that the
> potential that Heaven confers on them varies like this. They
> are like this because of what sinks and drowns their hearts.

Poverty, starvation, hunger, political injustice: all these things, as far as Mencius is concerned, risk leading to discontent, unhappiness, lack of virtue, and the arising of violence. It's not that Mencius is claiming that there's no internal dimension to happiness, flourishing or virtue – he says that 'most' young men in times of poverty become violent, but not 'all' – but he does remind us that these things depend strongly upon external conditions. For a ruler to rule badly is for them to preside over a state in which there's inequality, poverty, and the absence of those things that nurture human flourishing; and in such circumstances, we simply can't expect the people who suffer these conditions to act well.

For Mencius, it's useless to claim that those who live in poverty, who suffer severe injustice, or who are hungry, should nevertheless take full moral responsibility for their lack of happiness and their lack of flourishing. To do so is a denial of political responsibility. Do you agree?

Mencius' book ends on a somewhat melancholy note. It is, he says, not much more than 100 years since the time of Confucius; and yet there's still no sign of a just society capable of fully supporting human happiness:

> It is not long from the era of a sage, and we are close to the home of a sage. Yet where is he? Where is he?

And even today, it can still seem as if we haven't yet found a way of organizing ourselves to fully encourage the development of human flourishing, to allow those sprouts of virtue to grow. So in the next and final section of the book we'll return to ask some questions about the place of happiness in the contemporary world.

Part III
Beyond Happiness

18. More to life?

In brief
Happiness, it begins to seem, is not one thing but many.
As a result, the various approaches to happiness explored
in this book are not all compatible. In this chapter we look
back over these various approaches and ask what are the
*implications of the idea that there may be **different kinds***
of happiness.

At the beginning, I said that this wasn't a book that aimed to provide you with the secret of happiness. Now that we've explored happiness in a wide variety of guises – from Zhuangzi dragging his tail in the mud to Aquinas' claim that true happiness lies only in God, from Epicurus' garden to the monastery of Śāntideva at Nālandā, and from the *stoa* of ancient Athens to the deforested Ox Mountain of ancient China – we can see why this might be. The various accounts of happiness that we've explored here are not all in harmony with each other. There are many kinds of happiness, in other words, and many forms of the good life. Attaining to Epicurean happiness is not the same thing as attaining to the happiness of the Stoics or of the Buddhists. To the extent that happiness is a possibility for followers of Zhuangzi and Confucius, the followers of these two thinkers are *differently happy*.

REMEMBER THIS!!! The different philosophical approaches to happiness we've been exploring here aren't necessarily different approaches to the same thing. There may be different kinds of happiness, and if we want to be happy, we may need to choose which kind of happiness we're interested in.

If you've tried out some of the practical exercises in this book, you may have discovered that it is indeed true that we can do things to help support our well-being (positive psychology), to nourish our lives (Zhuangzi), to free ourselves from the various disturbances of life (Epicureanism), to overcome irrational expectations that cause us distress (Stoicism), and so on. But you may also have discovered the various tensions between the differing conceptions of happiness.

TRY IT NOW! Look back over the various approaches to happiness in this book. Here's a brief summary of them to remind you:

Approach	Summary
Aristotle	Attaining to excellence by avoiding excess and deficiency.
Epicurus	Cultivating pleasure by choosing static over kinetic pleasures.

Approach	Summary
Cynicism	Living naturally and questioning conventional morality; becoming 'cosmopolitan'.
Stoicism	Understanding the nature of things, and according our expectations with necessity.
Aquinas	Recognizing the limitations of worldly happiness; divine grace as an aspect of happiness.
Buddhism	Understanding the causes of suffering. Meditation as a means of cultivating calm and insight.
Śāntideva	Altruism as a means to happiness not just for myself, but for others as well.
Confucius	Ritual as a way of bringing harmony and order to our lives.
Zhuangzi	Cultivating uselessness, so that we can better nourish our lives.
Mencius	Exploring the political and social conditions that help nurture the 'sprouts' of virtue.

Now ask yourself the following questions:

- Which of these approaches do you think is the most helpful?
- Which is the least helpful?
- Did you try any of the exercises? If so, which were the most useful, and which helped the least?

- Which two approaches to happiness do you think are the *least* compatible with each other? What is it that makes them incompatible?

A religion of happiness?

Many of the approaches to happiness explored in this book seem to imply that much of our happiness is *up to us*. But how much is it up to us? In the past, happiness was often seen as a matter of chance, an aspect of our experience that might befall us almost by accident (the root of the word 'happy' is 'hap', meaning 'chance' or 'luck', as in 'mishap'). But the proliferation of books claiming to reveal the secret of happiness suggests that the predominant view today is that happiness is almost entirely up to us. Somewhere along the way, it seems, happiness has been transformed not only into a project upon which we must embark, but also into a *right* that we possess, a *duty* we must fulfil, even a *religion* with its own creeds and orthodoxies and mantras and hopes of coming redemption.

However, when happiness becomes the ultimate goal of human life, we can begin to feel, if we aren't beaming away beatifically like those strange gods depicted in the author photographs on the back of self-help books, that somehow our life has gone wrong and we've failed in the rush towards earthly happiness. And yet, if happiness is not one kind of thing but many kinds of thing, and if these different conceptions of happiness may all be, in their way, desirable but not necessarily compatible, then the idea that there's such a thing as complete happiness and fulfilment must be a myth.

 Go to your nearest bookshop (or look online) and browse through the books on happiness. Give yourself at least twenty minutes to see what's on offer. Do these different books claim to offer the 'secret' of happiness? If so, what kind of happiness do they promise? And what do these books ask of the reader?

Now, thinking about the books as a whole, ask yourself if there is any truth in the idea that happiness has become a kind of religion. What might this claim actually mean?

The myth of perfect happiness

Sometimes, reading books about happiness, we can imagine that if only we were happy, all of our problems would be solved: we would become competent in any situation, resilient to all the world throws at us, able to rise above any misfortune. Books on happiness are often filled with such inspiring stories of overcoming the odds and remaining happy. However, not only may this idea of perfect happiness be *incoherent* (on the grounds that happiness can consist of a number of things, not all of which are compatible), it may also be *unkind*, because it demands of us something that's very likely impossible – and then adds to any misery we're already suffering the misery of knowing that we've failed in rising above it.

Seeing happiness as inherently limited, in other words, may allow us a greater happiness. In unburdening us from the perpetual demand to be happy, it frees us up to appreciate the various kinds of happiness that we *do* in fact experience, without seeing these kinds of happiness as in themselves deficient, as somehow not living up to our notions of perfect happiness. Kierkegaard talked about being *happy in his unhappiness*; but it's even more common perhaps that we find ourselves *unhappy in our happiness*, because of a dream of a greater happiness that lies somewhere over the horizon.

IF YOU REMEMBER ONE THING Partial happiness (and all happiness in this world, as Aquinas knew, is partial happiness) might be happiness enough. And when we recognize this fact, we can begin to see that there are many other things, *besides happiness*, that also matter, that might be worth considering as aspects of the good life.

This, then, is the subject of the next chapter.

19. Cutting happiness down to size

In brief
The question we'll be looking at in this chapter is this: What else, other than happiness, may matter in life? It's true that happiness is important to us; but it's also the case that happiness isn't the only thing that's important to us. Here we'll look at some of the other things that matter, and we'll be trying to cut happiness down to size, to see it as one good thing among many.

What else matters?
Many books on happiness start with the claim that we all want to be happy. And it's true that most of us, most of the time, do. But what's less frequently commented upon is the fact that this isn't the only thing that we want. There are many things that we may consider to be aspects of the good life – meaning, liberty, justice, knowledge and reason, for example – that aren't immediately reducible to, or even compatible with, our notions of happiness.

The point that not all good things are compatible is made by the philosopher Isaiah Berlin:

> To admit that the fulfilment of some of our ideals may
> in principle make the fulfilment of others impossible is

to say that the notion of total human fulfilment is a formal contradiction, a metaphysical chimera.

In other words, even if we think happiness is one of the more important things in human life, ultimately happiness must take its place alongside all the other things that we deem good: as something that's perhaps desirable, but not ultimately so; as something that can perhaps even be cultivated, but that can never be completely fulfilled.

Write a list of at least five things, other than happiness, that you think are desirable to human life. Now ask yourself which of these are compatible with each other, and which are incompatible. If they're incompatible, how are they incompatible? What does this mean for the place of happiness in human life?

The business of happiness

Happiness these days is big business. Increasingly, politicians talk about happiness, commission studies on the good life, and ask economists not just how to boost the economy but also how it might be possible to boost national happiness. There's much to be welcomed in these changes. Richard Layard points out (taking the notion of subjective well-being as a starting point) that, 'as Western societies have got richer, their people have become no happier'.

The notion within classical economics that increased wealth necessarily correlates with increased happiness has proved to be ill-founded. In the light of this, there's good reason that at the level of public policy, governments should be asking how to legislate not just for wealthier, but also for happier societies.

But is this change from a concern with wealth to a concern with happiness really as substantial as all that? For example, the happiness agenda is currently being marketed to businesses on the grounds that happier employees are more productive employees; and more productive employees generate even more wealth. So, on the one hand happiness is being offered as an *alternative* to the pursuit of wealth; but on the other hand, it's being suggested that happiness might be the very thing that fuels the creation of wealth: the question naturally arises whether this is really the substantial shift in values that it's claimed to be.

Contemporary discussions on happiness at the political level often oscillate between these two poles: happiness as a real alternative, and happiness as a means of supporting the endless generation of wealth and profit. But perhaps what's needed here is not so much a final decision between economic well-being and happiness, but instead an ability, now that we've started to broaden out the political discussion about what matters, to begin factoring in other things: not just wealth, nor just wealth and happiness, but wealth, happiness, justice, reason, equality, and so on. To do this, and to do it seriously, we might have to eventually concede that we can judge the success of a government not by wealth alone, nor even by wealth and happiness, but instead by a range of competing things, some of which may be deeply antithetical to our current ways of organizing ourselves.

 See if you can track down a newspaper article, a speech, or an account of a speech by a politician on the subject of happiness. Read or listen to the text and ask yourself the following questions:

- Why is the politician in question talking about happiness? What political purpose does this serve?
- What kind of idea of happiness is implied here?
- Which of the thinkers that we've explored seems most in harmony with this idea of happiness?
- Are there any philosophical, political or ethical problems with the idea of happiness that's being proposed? If so, what are they?

Subversive happiness?

One reason we might continue to need a *philosophical* approach to happiness, rather than becoming fixated only on the idea of subjective well-being, is that it may remind us of the radical nature of some of the ideas of happiness that have existed throughout history. And while we can cautiously welcome some aspects of the growing political concern with happiness, there are reasons to remain at least a little sceptical.

Today, happiness programmes are being run everywhere from schools to workplaces to the military. The positive psychology language of character strengths, virtues and 'resilience' – the ability to deal with adversity – is found not just within psychology departments and universities, or within the pages of books on happiness, but has become part of a broader political conception of the good life. Soldiers are trained to develop 'resilience' on the field of battle and 'spiritual fitness' to help them deal with the trauma of war; employees are asked to respond to increased demands from their managers by using techniques drawn from positive psychology; and happiness is increasingly considered to be an aspect of citizenship.

THINK ABOUT IT

But what if you begin to suspect that the war that you're fighting, or the things you're being asked to do in the course of this war, are profoundly unethical? What if the demands of your managers are unreasonable and damaging? What if, like Diogenes, you look at the prevailing values that are being promoted as 'citizenship' and you see a measure of hypocrisy and double-speak, and you begin to suspect that the coin of conventional morality needs re-minting?

If we care about the kind of world we live in, we need to be able to ask the more difficult questions about the values that underlie our political systems, and we need to continue to explore the broader questions of the kind of society we're interested in bringing about. It has been claimed, not without injustice, that the happiness agenda risks becoming socially conservative, and is increasingly pressed into the service of governments that wish to avoid more difficult questions of ethics, social responsibility and inequality. To avoid this happening, it will help to do two things: firstly, to keep alive the awareness that there are other things that matter, besides happiness; and secondly, to recognize that as much as the notion of happiness may serve current agendas, it may also subvert them.

IF YOU REMEMBER ONE THING If we really care about happiness, not just for ourselves but as a general principle, then we can't ignore questions of injustice and inequality. And so, if we're to enter into the current debates about happiness, we need to be informed not only by a richer philosophical view of happiness, but also by a sense of what else may matter.

20. Cockaigne

In brief
In this final chapter, we look at the utopian dreams that
human beings have had of perfect worlds; and we ask how
much happiness, in the end, it's reasonable to hope for.

Back in the Middle Ages, while Thomas Aquinas dictated
his works to the patient scribes, the peasantry of Europe
laboured in the fields and returned home to dream of happier worlds. And one of their most enduring dreams was
that of a land of absolute happiness, a realm where toil
and suffering were no more: the Land of Cockaigne. In this
wonderful place, ready-cooked pigs ran around with knives
already strapped to them, so that people could chop off
chunks. Roast ducks obligingly placed their heads on plates
so that they could be eaten. Eggs with legs walked up to
people, ready to be consumed. When it rained, it rained
cheese. There were tables laden with food and wine under
which you could lie, simply waiting for good things to drop
into your mouth. And as for the sex, in Cockaigne even the
monks and nuns were willing to show you a good time.

This kind of vision was common not only in Europe
but elsewhere. In America, there was the Big Rock Candy
Mountain; in the Buddhist traditions there were the pure
lands and the heavenly realms; and China had its fair share

of Daoist and Buddhist-inspired lands of happiness. The Confucians were more sober and less mystical, but even Confucius looked back to an earlier era that he believed to have been one of almost perfect harmoniousness, and dreamed of a future time in which such an era might be re-established.

Perhaps, however, we aren't made to live in Cockaigne, as Schopenhauer recognized:

> Imagine a race transported to a Utopia where everything grows of its own accord and turkeys fly around ready-roasted, where lovers find one another without any delay and keep one another without any difficulty: in such a place some men would die of boredom or hang themselves, some would fight and kill one another, and thus they would create for themselves more suffering than nature inflicts on them as it is.

Happy place and no place

The happiness of Cockaigne, although it might be attractive at first glance, feels somehow impoverished. Even the various utopian visions of happiness found in the world's religions – the heavenly realms, the lotus flowers, the veiled promises of curiously spiritualized sexual delight, the end-less muzak played on the harp – often seem to present us with a restrictive kind of happiness.

While Schopenhauer may not be right in his gloomy assessment that happiness is all but impossible, he is astute in pointing out the absurdity of utopian dreams.

KEY TERM

Utopia was a term coined by Thomas More (1478–1535), and can be read either as *eu*-topia, which means 'happy place', or *u*-topia, which means 'no place'. This suggests that we should be careful about staking everything on dreams of utopia.

But this is no reason to be entirely cheerless. Whether we understand it in terms of *hedonia* or *eudaimonia*, happiness in its various forms is often something we want, sometimes something we seek, or something we want or seek on behalf of others, and something we often, but not invariably, deem to be good. Happiness matters. *Of course* it matters. But perhaps it doesn't always matter as much as we think it does. And if we're to flourish at all, if we're to find fulfilment in the world, if pleasures matter to us, then it's here, in a world far from utopia, that we can find these things, puzzling and contradictory though they may sometimes be.

TRY IT NOW!

As a final exercise, try to think of any contemporary visions of utopia or the Land of Cockaigne. These might be religious, they might be political, or they might be personal. Now answer the following questions:

- How attainable, if at all, do you think these kinds of utopia are?
- Would you want to live in this kind of utopia?
- What might the disadvantages of such a utopia be?
- Would such a utopia actually provide the happiness that it promised?

Further reading

The literature on happiness is vast and grows not just by the day but by the hour. It's impossible to keep up with everything that's published on the subject. The following section aims to give you a sense of some of the more interesting books and ideas.

All of the books recommended here are available on the general market. There's also a lot of scholarly research on happiness – there's even a *Journal of Happiness Studies*, which is filled with excellent articles. However, scholarly articles can be hard (and, more to the point, expensive) to track down for the general reader, so I've focused on those books and articles that are more widely accessible.

Introduction: The passage from Kierkegaard comes from his later papers dated 24 August 1849, and is reprinted in the entry for 1841, the year of Kierkegaard's decision not to marry, in the sadly out of print (but still relatively easy to track down) *The Journals of Kierkegaard 1834–1854* (Fontana). Some good general books on happiness are as follows: economist Richard Layard's *Happiness: Lessons from a New Science* (Penguin); *The Happiness Equation* by Nick Powdthavee (Icon); Darrin McMahon's *The Pursuit of Happiness* (Penguin); Sissela Bok's *Exploring Happiness: From Aristotle to Brain Science* (Yale); Daniel Nettle's brief but informative *Happiness: the Science Behind your Smile* (Oxford) and the companion volume by Dylan Evans,

Emotion: the Science of Sentiment (also published by Oxford); *The Happiness Hypothesis* by Jonathan Haidt (Arrow); *Stumbling on Happiness* by Daniel Gilbert (Harper Perennial); and Richard Schoch's *The Secrets of Happiness* (Profile).

Chapter 1: Schopenhauer's thoughts on happiness can be found in *Essays and Aphorisms* (Penguin).

Chapter 2: The Kant passage comes from *The Grounding for the Metaphysics of Morals*. There are several translations, including the one included in the collection *Ethical Philosophy* (Hackett).

Chapter 3: For positive psychology, read Martin Seligman's *Authentic Happiness* (Nicholas Brealey Publishing) and Jonathan Haidt's *The Happiness Hypothesis* (Arrow). Or visit authentichappiness.com

Chapter 4: More on the Satisfaction With Life Scale (SWLS) can be found on the Authentic Happiness website (see the weblinks section). *Utilitarianism and Other Essays* (Penguin) is a good collection and includes extracts from Bentham.

Chapter 5: Pierre Hadot's *Philosophy as a Way of Life* (Blackwell) is an interesting, if complex, exploration of philosophy and ancient experiments in living. Mill's autobiography is widely available in various editions.

Chapter 6: Among the books that take a broader approach to happiness, one of the best is Richard Schoch's *The Secrets of Happiness* (Simon & Schuster).

Chapter 7: Aristotle's *Nicomachean Ethics* is readily available in various editions.

Chapter 8: It's relatively easy to get hold of the collected writings of Epicurus. I've used *The Essential Epicurus* (Prometheus Books). There's also an edition called *The Epicurus Reader* published by Hackett.

Chapter 9: An excellent source for Cynicism is William Desmond's book *Cynics* (Acumen).

Chapter 10: There are several translations of the *Enchiridion* available, including one by Dover Thrift Editions, one from Prometheus Books, and a full translation in Michael Morgan's bumper *Classics of Moral and Political Theory* (Hackett). Other Stoic books, such as Marcus Aurelius' *Meditations*, are readily available.

Chapter 11: The essay on Thomas Aquinas by Umberto Eco is in *Faith in Fakes: Travels in Hyperreality* (Vintage). For the extracts from Aquinas that concentrate on happiness, read *Treatise on Happiness* translated by John A. Oesterle (Notre Dame University Press)

Chapter 12: Matthieu Ricard has written an introduction to happiness from a more or less Buddhist perspective simply called *Happiness* (Atlantic). There are innumerable introductions to Buddhism available, but for brevity and clarity Michael Carrithers' *The Buddha* (Oxford) remains worth reading.

Chapter 13: For a good, contemporary introduction to meditation in the Buddhist tradition, try *Change Your Mind: A Practical Guide to Buddhist Meditation* by Paramananda (Windhorse Publications). The material on the research into meditation and happiness comes from Owen Flanagan's *The Really Hard Problem* (MIT Press).

Chapter 14: For Śāntideva, one of the most accessible translations is the Oxford World Classics version of *The Bodhicaryāvatāra* (Oxford).

Chapter 15: For Chinese thought in general, an excellent place to start is Sarah Allan's *The Way of Water and the Sprouts of Virtue* (SUNY). Roger Ames and Henry Rosemont have produced a good philosophical translation of Confucius called *The Analects of Confucius: A Philosophical Translation* (Ballantine Books).

Chapter 16. There are lots of translations of Zhuangzi or Chuang-tzu. Burton Watson's *Chuang-tzu, the Inner Chapters* (Hackett) is a classic; and there's a more recent translation by Brook Ziporyn (Hackett). The book by François Jullien from which the quote comes is *Vital Nourishment: Departing from Happiness* (Zone Books).

Chapter 17. Bryan W. Van Norden's translation of Mencius, *Mengzi: With Selections from Traditional Commentaries* (Hackett) is elegant and clear. For Mencius in particular it's worth reading Sarah Allan's book as well (see above).

Chapter 18: Recent criticisms of what I have called 'the religion of happiness' include *Smile or Die: How Positive Thinking Fooled America and the World* by Barbara Ehrenreich (Granta) and *Perpetual Euphoria: On the Duty to be Happy* by Pascal Bruckner (Princeton).

Chapter 19. Isaiah Berlin's essays are collected together as *The Proper Study of Mankind* (Pimlico). The *Journal of Happiness Studies* is the place to find a lot of the debate about happiness.

Chapter 20. The quote, again, comes from the Penguin translation of Schopenhauer's *Essays and Aphorisms*. There's a book-length study of the Land of Cockaigne called *Dreaming of Cockaigne* written by Herman Pleij (Columbia University Press).

Websites

The following websites may be useful or interesting.

Authentic Happiness: The UPenn positive psychology website, with lots of questionnaires and activities (requires free login): http://www.authentichappiness.sas.upenn.edu/

Action for Happiness: A 'movement for positive social change': http://www.actionforhappiness.org/

The 'Are You Happy?' Project: An interesting global project asking participants the simple question: 'Are you happy?': http://theareyouhappyproject.org/

Philosophy Bites: A good philosophy website and podcast with some material on happiness and on the philosophers covered here: http://www.philosophybites.com/

The Happiness Formula: A webpage and set of resources from the BBC: http://news.bbc.co.uk/1/hi/programmes/happiness_formula/

Index

209

Notes

You can use the following pages to make your own notes on any of the exercises in the book.

Notes

Notes

Notes

Notes